The

ENCYCLOPEDIA

of

Crystals, Herbs, & New Age Elements

ADAMS MEDIA

An A to Z Guide to New Age
Elements and How to Use Them

D0584810

Adams Media
New York London Toronto Sydney New Delhi

Adams Media
An Imprint of Simon & Schuster, Inc.
100 Technology Center Drive
Stoughton, MA 02072

For information about special discounts for bulk purchases, please contact Simon &
Schuster Special Sales at 1-866-506-1949 or business@simonandschuster.com.

The Simon & Schuster Speakers Bureau can bring authors to your live event. For more
information or to book an event contact the Simon & Schuster Speakers Bureau at
1-866-248-3049 or visit our website at www.simonspeakers.com.

Manufactured in the United States of America

7 2021

Library of Congress Cataloging-in-Publication Data
The encyclopedia of crystals, herbs, and new
age elements.
      pages cm
   Includes index.
   ISBN 978-1-4405-9109-9 (pb) -- ISBN
978-1-4405-9110-5 (ebook)
1. Occultism--Encyclopedias. 2.
Crystals--Miscellanea--Encyclopedias.
3. Herbs--Miscellanea--Encyclopedias.
4. Flowers--Miscellanea--Encyclopedias.
5. Essences and essential oils--Miscellanea-
-Encyclopedias. 6. New Age movement--
Miscellanea--Encyclopedias. I. Adams Media
   BF1439.E53 2016
   133'.2--dc23
2015030435

ISBN 978-1-4405-9109-9
ISBN 978-1-4405-9110-5 (ebook)

Contents

7 The Power of Insight: Divination Systems, Tools, and Practices — 204

8 The Power of Symbols — 245

9 The Power of Movement — 253

10 The Power of Touch — 265

Introduction

New Age is a broad term that is used to describe an Eastern-influenced cultural movement that arose in the Western world in the 1970s. The New Age movement has many subcategories, including medicine, spirituality, and environmentalism, and it continues to thrive around the world today in countless constantly evolving forms.

If you've ever browsed around a New Age gift shop or bookstore, you've probably encountered a seemingly disconnected array of stones and crystals, herbs and spices, candles and incense, and books on topics ranging from astrology to yoga. Though these items all belong to disparate cultural traditions from different parts of the world at various points throughout human history, they are all part of the big New Age picture.

For thousands of years, stones, herbs, and other natural elements have been used in cultures across the globe to promote health and prosperity, provide protection, ease pain and suffering, and facilitate spiritual enlightenment. While modern advances in science and medicine have brought us invaluable medications, treatments, and therapies, many of the world's oldest remedies and practices are still widely used and considered highly effective.

Long before hospitals and pharmacies, there were plants. The first humans were hunter-gatherers who relied on the environment for survival. They learned which plants were toxic and which were beneficial, and they developed remedies for illness and discomfort that were honed and adapted over time. The same process occurred with other natural elements, from stones to scents. In ancient Egypt, stones and crystals collected from the earth were worn to draw sickness from the body. In ancient China, herbs and roots were used to treat ailments ranging from headaches to indigestion. Remains of incense dating back thousands of years have been found all over the world. All of these practices have persisted through history and continue to be used regularly in our modern lives.

In this book, New Age novices and aficionados alike will find some of the most treasured New Age elements and practices, organized into ten chapters: stones, herbs, flowers, scent, fire and light, sound, insight, symbols, movement, and touch. Each entry covers information on the origins and various uses of the item or practice being discussed, including physical, spiritual, and magical applications.

Many of the remedies and practices in this book belong to the tradition of holistic healing, a diverse field of alternative medicine that treats the whole person, not just a single ailment or condition. Practitioners of holistic medicine believe that a person is made up of parts and if one part isn't working properly, it has a negative effect on the whole. Holistic healthcare practices covered in these pages include herbal medicine, acupuncture, and massage.

Some of the items discussed in this book have feng shui uses. Feng shui is the ancient Chinese practice of arranging the objects in your environment in a way that facilitates a free flow of energy. The *bagua*, which means "eight-sided figure or octagon," is your feng shui map.

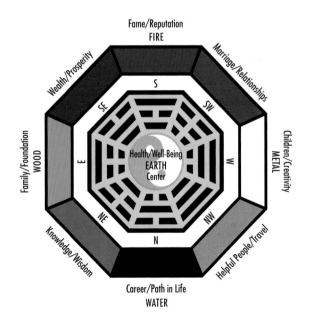

You may also see references to chakras throughout the book. In Hindu, yogic, and other traditions, the chakras are the energy centers in the body, arranged vertically along the spine. Each chakra governs a different kind of energy and connects to a different area of the physical body. The seven major chakras, from the top down, are:

- **Crown chakra:** Located at the top of the head, the crown chakra controls mental energy and is our connection to the divine.
- **Third-eye chakra:** This chakra, located between the eyes, is the seat of intuition. It governs our imagination, wisdom, and decision-making.
- **Throat chakra:** The throat chakra rules communication and expression, and is the source of personal truth.
- **Heart chakra:** This chakra is found in the middle of the chest and is all about love, joy, and inner peace.
- **Solar plexus or navel chakra:** This is the power chakra, the core self, located in the center of the abdomen.
- **Sacral or base chakra:** This is the pleasure center of the body, located in the lower abdomen, below the navel. It is the source of confidence and self-worth, and it also rules sexuality.
- **Root chakra:** Located at the base of the spine, this chakra is the foundation of the body and governs spiritual and physical grounding.

Some of the items found in these pages will be very familiar—you may already have them in your spice cabinet, garden, or backyard—but you'll learn new ways to use and enjoy them. Others may be totally new to you, and you may soon find yourself with a new hobby! Feel free to cherry-pick through the book and look up the items that most interest you. Curious about the healing powers of crystals? Check out Chapter 1. Looking for an herbal remedy for an ailment? Chapter 2 has you covered. Perhaps you're interested in some of the more magical New Age practices such as numerology or tarot (see Chapter 7). And what on earth is Rolfing, anyway? (Chapter 10 has the answer.) Be sure to check the glossary for any unfamiliar terms you find along the way.

Let this handy book be your go-to reference for all things New Age. As you read, remember that many of the items and practices in this book are very personal and the way they are experienced depends on the individual. What works for someone else will not necessarily work for you. Listen to your heart, body, and mind as you try out these New Age staples. Above all, enjoy the journey!

1

THE POWER OF STONES:
Crystals and Gemstones

Stones have been used for millennia to treat physical ailments and balance the energies of the body, as well as to facilitate mental, emotional, and spiritual well-being. They work through resonance and vibration, and through the minerals and other substances they contain. For example, the high concentration of copper in malachite can help reduce the swelling and inflammation that cause joint and muscle pain, and an analgesic called succinic acid is released when amber is warmed by the skin, making it helpful for treating arthritis and toothaches.

Stones can be found in two forms: raw and tumbled or polished. Raw stones are in their natural state, which means they may be sharp-edged or craggy and can be fragile. Tumbled or polished stones have been "tumbled" with fine sand or grit to smooth their edges. As a result of this process, tumbled stones are much more durable than raw stones and can be kept together (in a soft bag, for example), whereas raw stones should be kept separate to prevent scratching and breakage.

There are two main approaches to choosing a crystal or gemstone: You may be looking to treat a specific ailment or issue, or you may be simply searching for a stone that resonates with you. If you are completely new to the world of stones, your birthstone might be a great place to start. Otherwise, you can choose a stone by visiting a local store and browsing through its offerings. If a stone catches your eye, pick it up, hold it in your hand, and see how it feels. Trust your intuition. A stone that attracts your attention and feels right is the stone for you.

Agate

ORIGINS

Agate is a form of chalcedony, which is a variety of quartz. Agates form in cavities in volcanic rock. Water and carbon dioxide bubble out of the volcanic rock and rise to the surface, and over time the minerals crystalize in layers. This is why agates generally have a banded appearance, with layers of different colors. Agate is found all over the world but was named for the Achates River (now the Dirillo River) on the island of Sicily, Italy, where agates were first found.

HISTORY/LORE

The use of agate goes back to the Neolithic era, when it was favored for both healing and ornamentation. The ancient Greeks had many uses for agate. For example, moss agate, which does not have the classic layered appearance but instead has colors and patterns that resemble plant life or landscapes, was considered helpful in ensuring a plentiful harvest. Many cultures throughout history have believed that wearing agates protects against tragedy and evil.

USES

Healing Uses: There are many varieties of agate, and they have a wide range of healing uses. Blue lace agate, named for its lavender-blue color and lace-like pattern, is a calming stone that is used to soothe headaches, digestive discomfort, and skin issues, especially eczema. Fire agate, whose iridescent rainbow colors are reminiscent of a flame, can increase circulation and battle lethargy and depression. Because of agate's connection with the throat chakra, it is often worn around the neck to soothe coughs, sore throats, and even dental issues.

Magical Uses: Agates exhibit both the strength of a stone and the fluidity of air and water, making them useful as balancing and grounding stones. They are excellent for stabilizing energy and combating negativity and bitterness. Agates are often used in ceremonies concerning love, healing, protection, and courage, and many believe that a person can tell only the truth when looking at an agate.

Feng Shui Uses: Because agates have a soothing quality, it's helpful to place them in any area of your home that would benefit from a gentle, calming influence. Different varieties of agate can be used for different purposes around the home. A blue lace agate can be helpful in the Health/ Well-Being and Wealth/Prosperity sectors of your home, while a fire agate can create energy in the Marriage/ Relationships sector, such as the bedroom.

Personal/Spiritual Growth:
Agates raise consciousness and awareness of the self, encouraging contemplation that can lead to deep spiritual understanding and growth. They also enhance mental function and improve concentration and analytical abilities, which can be helpful for problem solving. Additionally, agates can be used to boost confidence and are specifically helpful with public speaking, stuttering, and related issues.

Amber

ORIGINS

Contrary to its appearance, amber is neither a stone nor a crystal; it's actually fossilized tree resin. Trees secrete resin to heal wounds and protect themselves against disease, and over time the resin dries and hardens. Long after the tree is gone the resin remains, and over the course of millions of years it becomes amber. Amber deposits have been found in places all over the world, including Mexico, the Dominican Republic, and the coast of the Baltic Sea. Baltic amber is the most well-known variety.

HISTORY/LORE

Amber has long been used in jewelry and other types of ornamentation, and many cultures have believed it holds magical powers. The ancient Greeks used amber to promote good health and ward off evil. The Aztecs and the Maya burned it as incense. Today, in addition to its continued use in jewelry and other art objects, amber is also valuable in the field of science for the insects and plant life it often contains.

USES

Healing Uses: Amber contains an analgesic called succinic acid, which is released when it is warmed by the skin. For this reason, necklaces and bracelets of amber beads are worn to ease arthritis and joint pain, as well as to soothe teething pain in infants and young children. Amber is an ingredient in many ointments and creams for burns and insect bites, and it is also used in cosmetics to destroy free radicals associated with aging. Wearing amber opens the solar plexus chakra and balances the energy of the body.

Magical Uses: Because amber is warm to the touch and yellow or orange in color, it is believed to hold the power of the sun, absorbed by the ancient trees that produced it. Use amber in meditation to tap into the wisdom of our ancestors and remember past lives, or to improve memory and boost confidence.

Feng Shui Uses: Place a piece of amber in the Health/Well-Being sector of your home to support good health and create a feeling of balance and calm. In the northeastern area, amber encourages self-exploration and wisdom. Place amber in pairs in the southwestern area to strengthen relationships.

Personal/Spiritual Growth: Amber helps you connect to your inner wisdom, bridging the gap between your everyday self and your spiritual core. It brings out your innate talents and abilities and enhances creativity so that you may more easily achieve your goals. It can also be used for psychic or physical protection.

Amethyst

ORIGINS

Amethyst is a variety of crystalline quartz that ranges in color from violet to mauve. The color of the amethyst changes in response to heat; depending on the temperature, it can become a range of colors, from reddish brown to yellow and even colorless. The majority of the world's commercial citrine is actually heat-treated amethyst (see Citrine in this chapter). The most significant deposits of amethyst are found in southern Brazil, Uruguay, and Madagascar, and it is also found in parts of Germany and Russia.

HISTORY/LORE

According to legend, the Greek god of wine, Dionysus, once pursued a nymph named Amethyst, who wished to escape his advances. The nymph asked for the help of the goddess Diana, who transformed her into a clear crystal. When Dionysus saw what she had done, he threw wine angrily upon the crystal, giving it its purple color. The ancient Egyptians believed amethyst could assuage fear and guilt, and the Greeks and Romans used it for protection against over-indulgence in food and alcohol.

USES

Healing Uses: Amethyst strengthens the immune system and supports oxygenation in the blood. For headaches, rub an amethyst crystal on your forehead. Placing amethyst under your pillow combats insomnia and brings pleasant dreams, and it may also help you remember your dreams upon waking. Amethyst is often incorporated in treatments for alcohol and drug addictions.

Magical Uses: This purple crystal has calming effects, defending against stress and negative energy. Amethyst is connected to the third-eye chakra (located between the eyes), which is responsible for intuition, and the crown chakra (at the top of the head), which controls mental energy. Wear amethyst jewelry to heighten awareness and relieve mental tension. As a talisman, amethyst brings feelings of pure happiness and love.

Feng Shui Uses: Amethyst is often used in purification rituals and can be helpful in calming household turbulence. It can also bring change when needed. Place it in the northeastern area of your home to foster wisdom.

Personal/Spiritual Growth:
Amethyst is the birthstone for the month of February. It facilitates spiritual awareness and forges a connection to the inner self. It also protects against psychic danger, especially during spiritual exploration. It is great for use in meditation practices because it helps ease the transition to a meditative state and encourages focus.

Aquamarine

ORIGINS

Aquamarine is a blue-green, transparent variety of the mineral beryl, which is colorless in its pure form. The blue-green color of aquamarine is a result of the presence of iron in the crystal. The word *aquamarine* comes from the Latin *aqua marina*, meaning "seawater." The stone is quite common, with major deposits occurring in Brazil, and it has also been found in other parts of the world, including the United States.

HISTORY/LORE

Greek sailors believed aquamarine was the treasure of mermaids, and carried it for good luck and protection as well as to prevent seasickness on sea voyages. The crystal was believed to be especially powerful when immersed in water. The Romans used aquamarine to cure throat, liver, and stomach ailments. Aquamarine has long been used to counteract the forces of evil and win the favor of the spirits.

USES

Healing Uses: This crystal strengthens the cleansing organs of the body, including the liver, spleen, and kidneys. It is also associated with the throat and heart chakras. For this reason, wearing an aquamarine necklace can help regulate thyroid issues. Aquamarine can also be used to calm an overactive immune system and is therefore helpful with allergies. Place aquamarine crystals on the eyes for eye issues.

Magical Uses: Aquamarine is a calming and clarifying stone that is helpful for filtering out unwanted thoughts, clearing up confusion, and bringing closure. With the tranquilizing energy of the sea, aquamarine is ruled by the moon. To recharge and cleanse an aquamarine crystal, place it in water on the night of a full moon. The soothing quality of this stone makes it useful for calming fears and phobias.

Feng Shui Uses: Aquamarine uses water energy, which is characterized by stillness, quiet strength, and purification. Water energy is traditionally associated with the northern area of a room or home, making this a great place for aquamarine crystals. Use aquamarine in the Career/Path in Life sector to ensure balance as your life unfolds. In the southwestern area of the home, aquamarine can improve troubled relationships.

Personal/Spiritual Growth: Aquamarine is the birthstone for the month of March. It is a great relaxation and meditation stone. When meditating with aquamarine, imagine yourself standing before a pool of clear, blue water. Release any negative emotions into the water and watch them float away. Aquamarine is also helpful for focusing energy toward the accomplishment of goals.

Aventurine

ORIGINS

Aventurine is a variety of quartz with inclusions of mica and other minerals that give it a sparkling appearance. The stone can be opaque or semi-translucent and is commonly green in color; other colors include blue, brown, and peach. The name *aventurine* comes from the French *aventure*, meaning "accident," pertaining to either its discovery or the randomness of the inclusions found in the stone. Deposits are found in Brazil, Austria, Russia, India, and Tanzania.

HISTORY/LORE

The ancient Tibetans prized aventurine and often used it for the eyes of their statues, believing it improved sight and creativity. In many cultures, aventurine is considered an opportunity stone that brings good luck in any situation, from a first date to a job interview. It is especially associated with money and games of chance, making it a favorite among gamblers. Many also believe that aventurine can guard against environmental and electromagnetic pollution.

USES

Healing Uses: Green is the color of healing, and green aventurine is considered an all-purpose healing stone. Specifically, it is associated with eyesight and is therefore helpful to people with near- or far-sightedness or astigmatism. It is also associated with the heart chakra, making it an excellent stone for people with cardiac or circulatory problems. Wearing a necklace with an aventurine pendant places the stone near the heart and increases its benefits.

Magical Uses: Aventurine is a very positive stone. It helps dissolve stress, anger, and anxiety, and produces an overall sense of harmony and calm. It is especially useful when getting over a disappointment or heartbreak, as it introduces a feeling of lightness and an understanding that everything in life is temporary.

Feng Shui Uses: Green aventurine uses wood energy, traditionally associated with the eastern and southeastern areas of a space as well as the Family/Foundation sector of the home. Wood energy encourages growth and new beginnings, and it also enhances vitality and abundance.

Personal/Spiritual Growth: Aventurine has a stabilizing effect on the mind and encourages perseverance in difficult times. It is helpful in letting go of old habits and disappointments, and moving into the future. The stone encourages optimism and increases motivation, helping you to achieve your goals. Meditating with aventurine can be helpful during times that feel stagnant.

Calcite

ORIGINS

Calcite is the most common form of calcium carbonate, the major mineral in limestone, marble, and chalk. It is colorless or white in its pure form but may be almost any color—pink, red, orange, yellow, green, blue, brown, black, or gray—when impurities are present. Calcite is very soft (a 3 on the Mohs scale) and can be easily scratched, so it is rarely used in jewelry. However, it is frequently used as a component in construction materials such as cement, mortar, floor tiles, and countertops, as well as paints and fertilizers. The clearest form of calcite is called Iceland spar, because it is common in Iceland. Calcite is also found in England, Italy, Germany, Romania, Mexico, and the United States.

HISTORY/LORE

Calcite gets its name from the Latin *calx*, meaning "lime." The ancient Egyptians favored it as an artisan material because of its softness and workability, and used a harder, banded variety of calcite called alabaster (distinct from the gypsum form of alabaster) to make ornamental and ceremonial objects such as sculptures and cosmetic containers.

USES

Healing Uses: Due to its acid-neutralizing effects, calcium carbonate is the major active ingredient in most commercially available antacid tablets, including Rolaids and TUMS. Calcite crystals can be used to encourage calcium absorption or to dissolve areas of calcification in the body, making them useful for treating bone problems such as osteoporosis and even bone cancer. Green calcite stimulates the immune system and battles bacterial infections. Iceland spar, also called optical calcite, soothes the tension that causes migraines.

Magical Uses: Pink calcite is powerful for releasing fear and grief and clearing a path for forgiveness. Blue calcite is a soothing stone that aids in recuperation and relaxation. It is also associated with the throat chakra and therefore aids in communication. Black calcite is helpful in past-life regression and recalling memories with the goal of letting go of the past. It also serves to alleviate depression and stress following a traumatic experience.

Feng Shui Uses: This is a great stone to have anywhere in your home, as it removes negative energies from the environment around it. Calcite is especially helpful in the Marriage/Relationships sector, particularly when a relationship is imbalanced or there is a disagreement.

Personal/Spiritual Growth: Calcite is a powerful energy cleanser and a stabilizing stone. It can be used to calm the mind, connect with the intellect, and boost emotional intelligence. It also enhances learning abilities, making it a wonderful stone for students. Red calcite removes emotional barriers that prevent forward movement in life. Yellow or golden calcite is helpful in meditation, as it encourages a deep state of relaxation and opens the mind to spiritual guidance.

Carnelian

ORIGINS

Carnelian is a variety of chalcedony that ranges in color from pink to reddish orange to brownish red. The color is a result of iron impurities in the crystal. Natural carnelian is increasingly rare, and many of the carnelian crystals on the market are actually agates that have been dyed and heat-treated. Agates masquerading as carnelian stones will have a striped appearance when held up to the light, while natural carnelian will have a more consistent, cloudy appearance. In addition to jewelry, carnelian is used for cameos and intaglios. The most significant source of carnelian is India, but it is also found in the United States, Peru, Brazil, Uruguay, and Madagascar.

HISTORY/LORE

The ancient Egyptians considered carnelian sacred and buried their dead with the stone to protect them on their journey to the afterlife. The ancient Greeks and Romans wore it to protect against sin. The prophet Muhammad is said to have worn a silver ring with an engraved carnelian stone on the little finger of his right hand, making it an important stone for Muslims. The emperor Napoleon famously wore an octagonal carnelian ring that he found in the sands of Egypt.

USES

Healing Uses: Due to its red color and iron content, this stone is associated with the blood; it can be used to cleanse the blood, stanch excessive blood flow, and heal open wounds. It also increases fertility and is beneficial during childbirth. Use carnelian stones to improve vitamin and mineral absorption, and to ensure adequate blood supply to the organs and tissues of the body. Carnelian connects with the sacral chakra, located between the navel and the pubic bone, which is the pleasure center of the body.

Magical Uses: Carnelian is a great stone to use in past-life regression or in the search for a "twin soul" or family. Its association with the element of fire makes it helpful for rekindling passion or romance. Carnelian can also be used to cleanse other stones.

Feng Shui Uses: Carnelian uses fire energy, bringing warmth, illumination, and passion to a space. This stone is associated with the southern area of a home or room, as well as with the Fame/Reputation sector. Keep carnelian near the front door of your home to secure protection and welcome abundance, and use it as an accent in a room where a boost of energy is needed.

Personal/Spiritual Growth:
This stone promotes peace and protects against negative emotions, both internal and external. It grounds its owner in the present reality and encourages acceptance while banishing envy, rage, and resentment. Carnelian also combats laziness and energizes its owner. Those looking for motivation and a creativity boost will be well served by this stone.

Chalcedony

ORIGINS

Chalcedony is a microcrystalline type of quartz and a broad category that includes some of the other stones in this chapter, such as agate, carnelian, and onyx. "True" or "actual" chalcedony is the milky white, gray, or blue variety of the stone, which often has a glowing, translucent quality. The stone is found all over the world, including the United States, Mexico, Brazil, Uruguay, India, and Madagascar. The name *chalcedony* is most likely derived from *Chalcedon*, an ancient Greek city in Asia Minor.

HISTORY/LORE

Chalcedony has been in use going back to the Bronze Age, when it was favored for carving seals, intaglios, and rings and other jewelry. The Roman orator Cicero is said to have worn a blue chalcedony stone around his neck due to its reputation for being beneficial during public speaking. The Native Americans believed chalcedony to be sacred and used it in spiritual ceremonies.

USES

Healing Uses: This stone promotes mineral absorption and prevents mineral buildup in the body, and it can also be used to support lactation in breastfeeding mothers. Additionally, chalcedony is said to lessen the effects of dementia and Alzheimer's. Blue chalcedony is associated with the throat chakra, making it effective for treating sore throats and other ailments of the neck area.

Magical Uses: Chalcedony is a nurturing stone often used to inspire goodwill and stabilize relationships, as well as to assist in telepathy and thought transmission. It absorbs and dissipates negative energy, paving the way for openness, generosity, and joy. Wear chalcedony for protection while traveling or to prevent bad dreams. Blue chalcedony can be used in weather magic and for treating illnesses associated with changes in the weather.

Feng Shui Uses: Blue chalcedony uses water energy, which is associated with the northern area of a home or room and the Career/Path in Life sector. Use blue chalcedony to calm, purify, and strengthen a space, especially one used for reflection or prayer.

Personal/Spiritual Growth: Chalcedony is often called the "speaker's stone," used to ease self-doubt and facilitate clear communication. It is especially helpful to actors, singers, salespeople, and others whose voices play a central role in their lives or careers. Blue chalcedony in particular is a creative stone that opens the mind to new ideas, enhances listening skills, and improves memory.

Citrine

ORIGINS

Citrine is a variety of crystalline quartz that ranges in color from pale yellow to reddish brown depending on its origin and whether it is natural or heat-treated. Natural citrine, found in Spain, France, Russia, Madagascar, and the Congo, is quite rare. Most commercial citrine is actually heat-treated amethyst, much of which comes from Brazil.

HISTORY/LORE

Citrine has been in use for thousands of years. It was used as a decorative gem during the Hellenistic period in ancient Greece, and some biblical scholars believe citrine is the tenth of twelve stones in Aaron's breastplate in the Book of Exodus. Citrine jewelry was very popular during the Victorian and Art Deco eras, when it was commonly used in pendants and brooches.

USES

Healing Uses: This crystal aids in digestion, stimulates circulation, and regulates the metabolism. It also relieves depression, anger, and mood swings. Citrine is also helpful in removing toxins, which is why it is often used in overcoming addictions. Wear citrine in contact with the skin of the fingers or the throat for best results.

Magical Uses: Citrine is a success and prosperity crystal. It combats negative energy and paves the way for growth. Use citrine to manifest abundance, both physically and spiritually. Carry a citrine crystal in your wallet or purse to attract money or curb overspending, or incorporate citrine while meditating on your goals to achieve abundance in the broader sense. Citrine can also be used as an "aura protector," warning against oncoming threats.

Feng Shui Uses: Place citrine in the Wealth/Prosperity area of your home or business, such as in the cash box. If nightmares or sleep disturbances are a problem, put a piece of citrine under your pillow at night to encourage a good night's sleep.

Personal/Spiritual Growth: Along with topaz, citrine is the birthstone for the month of November. It is associated with the solar plexus chakra, which is the power chakra, the core self. Wearing a long necklace with a citrine pendant will stimulate this chakra (located in the abdomen between the ribcage and the navel) and encourage creativity. Meditating with citrine facilitates access to inner thought. Wearing citrine raises self-esteem and combats destructive tendencies.

Clear Quartz

ORIGINS

Clear quartz, also called rock crystal, is a hard mineral composed of silicon dioxide, which is present in a variety of rocks, including sandstone and granite. It is the second most abundant mineral on Earth after feldspar and is located all over the world. Its abundance is attributed to its stability at a wide range of pressures and temperatures within the earth and its resistance to physical weathering once it has surfaced. The origin of the word *quartz* is unknown (although it may come from the Slavic word for "hard"), but the word *crystal* comes from the Greek word *krustallos*, meaning "ice." Clear quartz crystal comes in many forms, including tumbled stones, pillars or points, and clusters. Natural clear quartz is not to be confused with lead crystal, such as Swarovski, which is manmade.

HISTORY/LORE

According to an ancient Japanese creation myth, quartz formed from the breath of the revered white dragon and was believed to represent perfection. The Australian Aborigines used quartz in their rain and cleansing rituals. Crystal balls made of clear quartz have been used to divine the future since the Middle Ages, possibly earlier.

USES

Healing Uses: Quartz is an all-purpose healing stone that amplifies healing energy. It gets its power from its helical spiral crystalline form and piezoelectric quality. Quartz crystals can be used for any condition, but they are especially effective for stimulating the immune system and cleansing the organs. Placing quartz crystals on the body clears blockages. Acupuncture needles coated in quartz are said to increase the effectiveness of the procedure.

Magical Uses: Quartz crystals typically have six facets, which represent the six chakras from the root to the third eye, with the point of the crystal representing the crown chakra. This crystal works to increase consciousness, aids in past-life recall, and attracts love. Place clear quartz in bathwater to remove negative energy from the body.

Feng Shui Uses: In feng shui, clear quartz is valued for its ability to hold and emanate light, as well as to cleanse or purify the energy in a space. A clear quartz cluster or crystal ball placed in the living room will bring harmony to the home. Do not place a clear quartz cluster near your bed, as it can bring too much energy to the space and prevent restful sleep.

Personal/Spiritual Growth: Clear quartz is both colorless and contains every color of the rainbow, and therefore works on all levels of being. It removes negative energy and promotes clarity of thought. Use clear quartz during meditation to filter out distractions. Wearing or carrying clear quartz opens the heart and mind to the wisdom of the spirit realm.

Diamond

ORIGINS

Diamond is a crystalline form of carbon that is usually colorless but can also be yellow, blue, brown, or pink. It is the hardest of the gemstones, rating a 10 on the Mohs scale, and not nearly as rare as the jewelry industry suggests. Diamonds are found in many parts of the world, including Africa, Australia, Brazil, Canada, India, Russia, and the United States. The word *diamond* comes from the Greek *adamas*, meaning "hard" or "unconquerable," which evolved into the word *adamant.*

HISTORY/LORE

Diamond was first mined in India as early as the fourth century B.C.E., and the stone eventually made its way to European markets. By the 1400s, members of Europe's elite were donning diamond accessories. In the early 1700s, Brazil established itself as a major diamond source, and in the late 1800s large diamond deposits were discovered in South Africa. In 1888, British businessman Cecil Rhodes founded De Beers Consolidated Mines Limited with mines in South Africa, and by 1900 De Beers controlled 90 percent of the world's rough diamond production. It was De Beers that introduced the idea of the diamond engagement ring, with the slogan "a diamond is forever" appearing in the 1940s.

USES

Healing Uses: Diamond detoxifies and purifies the body, balances the metabolism, and aids in the treatment of allergies and chronic conditions. It is also beneficial for eye-related conditions, especially glaucoma, as well as dizziness and vertigo. Use diamond to improve the function of the brain, nerves, and sensory organs, or to combat aging and boost energy levels.

Magical Uses: Diamond is one of the few crystals that never need to be recharged; instead, it can be used as a support stone, amplifying the powers of other minerals. This stone increases the energy of everything it comes in contact with, but beware; it can also increase negative energy. Use a diamond to shine a light on anything negative that requires transformation.

Feng Shui Uses: Diamond is an ideal prism, both colorless and containing all the colors of the rainbow. Hang a diamond crystal in any window of your home to harness the sun's power and disperse light and energy freely throughout the space. Diamond is especially powerful in the Marriage/Relationships sector of the home.

Personal/Spiritual Growth: Diamond is the birthstone for the month of April. This stone clears fear and pain and encourages fortitude. It is especially useful for creative individuals, as it stimulates the imagination and inspires inventiveness. Diamond also cleanses and stimulates the crown chakra, which is the connection to the divine. Meditate with diamond to clear any debris from around your inner light, allowing it to shine outward.

Emerald

ORIGINS

Emerald is a variety of beryl that owes its green color to the presence of the metallic element chromium and sometimes vanadium. The color ranges from light to dark green, and it can be either transparent or opaque. It is a relatively hard stone (7.5–8 on the Mohs scale), but inclusions can affect its durability. Emerald deposits have been found in Brazil, Columbia, Egypt, India, and the United States.

HISTORY/LORE

Emeralds were first mined in Egypt, as early as 330 B.C.E., and the ancient Egyptian ruler Cleopatra famously loved the stone. The Inca and Aztecs of South America considered emerald to be a holy stone, but when the Spanish conquistadors arrived in the sixteenth century they exploited those deposits for trading. One of the largest and most famous emeralds is the Mogul Emerald, measuring 217.80 carats and about 10 centimeters high. Dating from 1695, this stone is inscribed with Islamic prayers on one side and engraved with flowers on the other. In 2001, it was auctioned off at Christie's of London to an anonymous buyer for $2.2 million.

USES

Healing Uses: Emerald stimulates the heart chakra and has a healing effect on both the emotions and the physical heart. It is also beneficial for the eyes, lungs, spine, and muscles. Worn around the neck, emerald can ease the effects of epilepsy and seizures. Emerald also aids in recovery from infectious disease.

Magical Uses: Emerald enhances loyalty, unity, and unconditional love, but if the stone changes color it is a sign of unfaithfulness. Wear this stone to ward off negativity and encourage positive actions, but do not wear it constantly, as this can trigger negative emotions. Emerald is especially helpful for enhancing psychic abilities and clairvoyance.

Feng Shui Uses: In feng shui, the color green is associated with wood energy, which encourages growth and new beginnings and enhances vitality and abundance. Place emerald stones in the eastern and southeastern areas of a space as well as the Family/Foundation sector of the home to bring domestic bliss.

Personal/Spiritual Growth: Emerald is the birthstone for the month of May. Working through the heart chakra, this stone balances the emotions, strengthens the connection to the divine, and provides support on one's spiritual journey. Emerald is excellent for meditation, as it focuses intention, raises consciousness, and gathers wisdom; just be sure to use a clear and not an opaque variety of the stone for meditation.

Fluorite

ORIGINS

Fluorite, also called fluorspar, is a mineral composed chiefly of calcium fluoride that is often fluorescent under ultraviolet light and can be a variety of colors, including blue, green, purple, yellow, and brown, as well as colorless. The word *fluorite* comes from the Latin verb *fluor*, meaning "to flow," due to its low melting point. The stone is quite common worldwide, with deposits found in Canada, the United States, Mexico, England, Germany, and China, among other locations.

HISTORY/LORE

Fluorite has long been used as a flux to lower the melting point of raw materials in the production of steel and, more recently, aluminum. The phenomenon of fluorescence, first described by the mathematician and physicist George Gabriel Stokes in 1852, takes its name from fluorite. The stone's relative softness (4 on the Mohs scale) has made it popular for carving for thousands of years.

USES

Healing Uses: Fluorite is a powerful healing stone. It strengthens the bones and teeth, and also relieves pain associated with arthritis. Rubbing a fluorite crystal across the body toward the heart provides pain relief. Use fluorite to battle infections, viruses, and skin issues. Use blue fluorite for ear, nose, and throat problems. Yellow fluorite releases toxins, aids the liver, and benefits cholesterol levels.

Magical Uses: Fluorite cleanses the aura and the chakras, especially the throat and crown chakras. This stone also has powerful protective qualities, especially on the psychic level. Use it to distinguish true feelings from outside influence and psychic manipulation.

Feng Shui Uses: Fluorite is an excellent stone for feng shui, especially the green variety, which harnesses wood energy. Place green fluorite in the eastern and southeastern areas of a space as well as the Family/Foundation sector of the home to bring balance and understanding. Surround family photographs with green fluorite stones to mend broken relationships. Place fluorite near your computer to clear electromagnetic stress.

Personal/Spiritual Growth: Fluorite integrates spiritual energies and heightens intuitive powers. Use it in meditation to focus the mind and open the door to the subconscious. Students especially will benefit from this stone, as it enhances learning capabilities and concentration.

Garnet

ORIGINS

The term *garnet* encompasses a broad group of minerals that includes alman-dine (deep violet-red), andradite (green to brown or black), grossularite (pale green, pink, brown, or black), hessonite (brown or yellowish brown), melanite (black), pyrope (deep red), rhodolite (rose-red or pink), spessartite (orange and red to brownish red), and uvarovite (green). Garnet is a relatively hard stone (6.5–7.5 on the Mohs scale) and is found worldwide. The word *garnet* most likely comes from the Latin *granatum*, meaning "pomegranate."

HISTORY/LORE

Ancient Egyptian pharaohs wore red garnet necklaces in life and were en-tombed with them for the afterlife. The Romans wore signet rings of carved garnet and used them to stamp wax seals on important documents. It is said that garnet was the only source of light on Noah's ark.

USES

Healing Uses: Garnet is a regenerative healing stone. It purifies and energizes the blood, heart, and lungs, and assists in the absorption of vitamins and minerals. Almandine in particular is helpful for absorbing iron. Grossularite enhances fertility. Melanite strengthens bones and soothes arthritis pain. Spessartite can be used to treat lactose intolerance and calcium imbalances. Use uvarovite to reduce inflammation or fever.

Magical Uses: Garnet has a strong connection to the pituitary gland and the third-eye chakra, the seat of intuition. Placing a garnet, particularly hessonite, on the third eye assists with past-life recall. Wearing melanite around the neck unblocks the heart and throat chakras, allowing the truth to be spoken. Placing spessartite under the pillow wards off nightmares.

Feng Shui Uses: Garnet revitalizes, purifies, and balances energy. Place a garnet in the northwestern area of a space before going on a journey. Use it in the southwestern area for assistance with partnership issues, and in this case always use two stones.

Personal/Spiritual Growth:
Garnet is the birthstone for the month of January. This stone strengthens the survival instinct and is therefore helpful in a crisis or any situation where there seems to be no way out. Andradite stimulates creativity and dissolves feelings of isolation or alienation. Hessonite banishes feelings of guilt and inferiority and encourages self-respect. Pyrope brings stability and vitality. Rhodolite fosters contemplation, intuition, and inspiration.

Hematite

ORIGINS

Hematite is the mineral form of ferric oxide, one of the three main oxides of iron. It can be black, silver, or red, and typically has a shiny appearance. The word *hematite* comes from the Greek *haima*, meaning "blood," due to its high iron content and red color. Deposits are found in Canada, Brazil, England, Italy, Switzerland, and Sweden.

HISTORY/LORE

According to legend, large hematite deposits formed in locations where ancient battles were fought, as a result of blood being shed and seeping into the earth. The Native Americans used powdered hematite to make war paint. Today, ground hematite is still used to make pigments as well as a product called jeweler's rouge, which is used to polish metal.

USES

Healing Uses: Hematite strengthens the blood supply, encourages the formation of red blood cells, and aids in the absorption of iron. It is also helpful for treating circulatory problems and anemia, as well as cleansing the kidneys. Hematite also ensures that fractures heal properly, and assists with spinal alignment (place it at the base and top of the spine for this), and it can draw heat from the body in the case of fever.

Magical Uses: Hematite is a grounding and protective stone that dissolves negativity. It strengthens our connection with the earth, particularly during out-of-body experiences, where it allows for safe travel and helps us bring back lessons to use in daily life.

Feng Shui Uses: Hematite is useful in the northern area of a space as well as the Career/Path in Life sector of the home. Place hematite in the corners of a room to create a protective spiritual grid. Carved hematite animals are excellent for feng shui, especially a turtle, which is one of the celestial animals of feng shui. For grounding on the go, keep tumbled hematite stones in your pocket, your car—just about anywhere!

Personal/Spiritual Growth: Hematite removes self-imposed limitations and boosts self-esteem and confidence. It is an excellent stone for overcoming compulsions and addictions, as it enhances willpower and survivability. Use hematite during meditation to calm your thoughts and bring focus and concentration.

Jade

ORIGINS

Jade comes in two forms: jadeite and nephrite. Jadeite is the harder, more highly valued form, and nephrite is softer and more common. Jadeite may be white, light to deep green, blue or blue-green, lavender, orange, or red, while nephrite can be found in creamy white, light to deep green, brown, and black varieties. Jadeite is found in Guatemala, Russia, China, and Myanmar (Burma), and nephrite is found in Guatemala, the Swiss Alps, Russia, China, and New Zealand.

HISTORY/LORE

Jade has been an important stone in China going back to the Neolithic period, when it was first used in burial rituals. During the Han dynasty (206 B.C.E. to C.E. 220), Chinese royalty were buried in jade burial suits to protect them in the afterlife. In Chinese culture, jade is believed to be a link between the physical and spiritual worlds and has long been prized as a carving stone to make jewelry, tools and weapons, and decorative and ceremonial objects.

USES

Healing Uses: Jade is a powerful cleansing stone that treats the filtration and elimination organs of the body, including the kidneys, spleen, and adrenal glands. It is helpful to the bones and joints, particularly the hips. Jade's restorative property assists in treating infections and helping stitched wounds to bind and heal properly, and it is also useful for fertility and childbirth.

Magical Uses: Jade is known as "the dream stone." It assists in remembering dreams and releasing suppressed emotions via dreaming. When placed on the forehead, it brings insightful dreams. More generally, jade aids in releasing negative thoughts and calming the mind. Wearing jade around the neck rebalances and unblocks the heart chakra, bringing self-acceptance to the wearer and harmony to dysfunctional relationships.

Feng Shui Uses: Jade uses wood energy, bringing growth, nourishment, and vitality to a space. Use it in the Family/Foundation and Wealth/Prosperity sectors of the home. Jade dragons, fish, and frogs symbolize the Chinese element of wood and springtime, and bring good luck and prosperity. Place these in the eastern area of the home for new beginnings and opportunity.

Personal/Spiritual Growth: Jade balances the personality and integrates the mind and body. It encourages you to be yourself and recognize that you are a spiritual being on a human journey. Jade prayer beads or beaded necklaces are useful in meditation. As a travel stone, jade protects against harm.

Jasper

ORIGINS

Jasper is an opaque microcrystalline type of quartz that comes in many varieties and is found worldwide. Its appearance varies widely due to the presence of organic material and mineral inclusions. Leopardskin jasper is named for its spotted look. The patterns of picture jasper look like paintings of landscapes or other scenes from nature. Rainforest jasper (also known as green rhyolite) has a mossy, earthy appearance. Red jasper's vibrant color is a result of its high iron content.

HISTORY/LORE

The ancient Egyptians carved jasper amulets and buried their dead with jasper for safe passage to the afterlife. In many cultures, jasper has long been known as the "rain bringer" and is used for the practice of dowsing (searching for water underground). Saint Hildegard of Bingen (1098–1179), a German nun, writer, composer, philosopher, and mystic, wrote of jasper's healing properties and recommended its use to relieve hay fever, cardiac arrhythmia, and temporary deafness.

USES

Healing Uses: Jasper is a regenerative healing stone. Leopardskin jasper provides support for the muscles and tendons as well as the bones, teeth, and hair. Both picture jasper and rainforest jasper stimulate the immune system and cleanse the kidneys and liver. Red jasper treats blood-related issues and encourages healthy pregnancy and birth.

Magical Uses: Jasper is called "the nurturing stone." Use leopardskin jasper to journey into other dimensions with the goal of personal transformation. Picture jasper is said to be the Earth Mother speaking to her children, sending messages from the past through its images. Rainforest jasper can be used to deal with past-life issues. Placed under the pillow, red jasper assists with dream recall.

Feng Shui Uses: Picture jasper and rainforest jasper use wood energy. Place these stones in the eastern area of a room to encourage growth and expansion. Red jasper uses fire energy, the energy of warmth, illumination, and activity, and is traditionally associated with the southern area of a home or room.

Personal/Spiritual Growth:
Leopardskin jasper grounds your spiritual practice and encourages you to stretch beyond your comfort zone in spiritual matters. Red jasper helps you clear your mind for prayer or meditation, and it increases focus and endurance during long spiritual ceremonies or practices.

Lapis Lazuli

ORIGINS

Lapiz lazuli is composed of several minerals, including lazurite, which gives it its intense blue color, as well as calcite and pyrite, which appear in the stone as white or gold flecks. *Lapis* is the Latin for "stone," and *lazuli* is from the Persian *lajward*, which is both the name of the stone in Persian and the place where it was mined. The word *azure*, which the American Heritage Dictionary defines as "a bright blue, as of a clear sky," derives from *lapis lazuli*. This stone is found in the United States, Chile, Argentina, Italy, Afghanistan, Pakistan, and Russia.

HISTORY/LORE

Modern-day Afghanistan was the source of lapis lazuli for the ancient Egyptian, Mesopotamian, Greek, and Roman civilizations. For thousands of years it has been carved to make jewelry and decorative and ceremonial objects, and powdered for use as a pigment. Lapis lazuli is one of the stones used in King Tutankhamun's 3,300-year-old gold burial mask, and the blue turban in Johannes Vermeer's *Girl with a Pearl Earring* (c. 1665) was painted with ultramarine pigment, made from powdered lapis lazuli.

USES

Healing Uses: Lapis lazuli soothes inflammation and provides pain relief, particularly for migraine headaches. It also treats the throat, larynx, and thyroid, and assists with ear issues, including hearing loss. Lapis lazuli supports the immune system and lowers blood pressure. For eye issues, rub the area with a lapis lazuli stone heated in warm water.

Magical Uses: Lapis lazuli opens the third eye and balances the throat chakra. Place this stone at the third eye to enhance psychic abilities, and wear it at the throat to facilitate communication and encourage truth telling. Lapis lazuli is excellent for meditation and spiritual journeying, as it brings harmony and deep inner knowledge.

Feng Shui Uses: This blue stone utilizes tranquil but powerful water energy, which is traditionally associated with the northern area of a home or room as well as the Career/Path in Life sector. Lapis lazuli is also effective in the Family/Foundation and Knowledge/Wisdom sectors of the home.

Personal/Spiritual Growth: Lapis lazuli is a truth stone. It encourages self-awareness and helps you discover and accept your innate truth. Hold a tumbled lapis lazuli stone in your hand and listen to your inner voice. Allow its cool, blue essence to release any agitation, frustration, or anger you may be holding inside.

Malachite

ORIGINS

Malachite is a green carbonate mineral that typically has a banded appearance and gets its color from its high copper content. Its name most likely derives from its resemblance to the leaves of the mallow plant. Malachite is quite common, with deposits found in Zambia, the Democratic Republic of the Congo, Romania, Russia, and the Middle East.

HISTORY/LORE

The ancient Egyptians wore malachite stones as adornments, and they also pulverized the stone and used the powder as eye shadow, as did the Greeks and Romans. In the Middle Ages, malachite was used to guard against the "evil eye" and to cure stomach ailments. Throughout history, many painters have used malachite as a pigment in their work, but that practice has fallen out of favor due to the stone's toxicity in powdered form.

USES

Healing Uses: Malachite is a powerful stone that must be handled with caution, preferably under the supervision of a qualified crystal therapist. Use malachite only in its polished form, as the dust of the raw form is toxic if inhaled or ingested. Malachite eases menstrual cramps and pain during childbirth, and it also reduces the swelling and inflammation that cause joint and muscle pain. Additionally, this stone treats asthma, lowers blood pressure, and enhances the immune system.

Magical Uses: This green stone amplifies positive energy and brings the heart chakra back into balance. It can also be used for scrying or for accessing other worlds. Place malachite on the third eye to enhance psychic vision.

Feng Shui Uses: Malachite absorbs negative energy and pollutants, particularly radiation, and should be cleansed frequently by placing it on a quartz cluster in the sun. Malachite uses wood energy and is most effective when placed in the eastern and southeastern areas of a home or room.

Personal/Spiritual Growth: Malachite is a stone of transformation; it encourages risk-taking and brings change. Place malachite on the solar plexus to absorb negative emotions and facilitate deep emotional healing. Place it on the heart to bring balance and harmony and foster unconditional love.

Obsidian

ORIGINS

Obsidian, also called volcanic glass, is molten lava that cooled so rapidly it had no time to crystallize. It has an opaque, shiny surface and is typically black but can also be brown, blue, green, red-black, silver, rainbow, or "gold sheen" if minerals or other inclusions are present. Other types of obsidian include Apache tears and snowflake obsidian. Obsidian is found worldwide wherever there is volcanic activity.

HISTORY/LORE

Because of its smooth, curved surface and sharp edges, obsidian has been used to make tools and weapons, especially arrowheads, for thousands of years. It is less common in jewelry because it is not that hard (5 on the Mohs scale) and is easily scratched. Apache tear obsidian gets its name from legend: The U.S. cavalry ambushed a group of Native Americans of the Apache tribe who were camped on a mountain. Three-quarters of the Apaches were killed within minutes, and those who remained, realizing they were outnumbered, chose to leap to their deaths rather than die at the hands of the white men. Their loved ones wept when they discovered their bodies at the base of the mountain, and black stones formed where their tears fell. The legend says that anyone who holds an Apache tear never needs to cry again, because the loved ones of those lost in the fight with the U.S. cavalry have already cried enough tears for all mourners.

USES

Healing Uses: Obsidian detoxifies the body, aids digestion, and dissolves blockages wherever they occur. It also alleviates the pain of arthritis, joint problems, cramps, and injuries. Apache tear obsidian assists with vitamin absorption. Snowflake obsidian improves circulation.

Magical Uses: Obsidian is a powerful, cathartic stone. It brings tamped-down negative emotions and unpleasant truths to the surface so they can be dealt with and released. This stone also facilitates past-life healing. A large piece of obsidian can be used to soak up environmental pollution. Obsidian placed by the bed or under the pillow draws out stress and tension, but once surfaced, the causes of these issues must be resolved. Apache tear or snowflake obsidian works best for this, and stones should be cleansed under running water after use.

Feng Shui Uses: Place obsidian in the northern area of a home or room for assistance with personal journeys. Place it in the Health/Well-Being sector for grounding and protection. Because obsidian draws in negative energy, it should be cleansed regularly and should not be placed anywhere where it will be forgotten or neglected.

Personal/Spiritual Growth: Obsidian helps you to face your inner darkness and integrate it into your life rather than burying it. Black obsidian balls are powerful for meditation and scrying, but they should be used by only those who can consciously process what they see and use the information for good. Place obsidian on the navel to ground spiritual energy in the body. Place it on the third eye to tackle mental barriers.

Onyx

ORIGINS

Onyx is a type of chalcedony quartz that has a banded or marble-like appearance and is relatively hard (6.5–7 on the Mohs scale). Most people think of onyx as a black stone, but it also occurs in gray, white, blue, brown, yellow, and red varieties. It is found in many parts of the world, including the United States, Mexico, Brazil, and Italy. The word *onyx* comes from the Greek *onux*, meaning "fingernail."

HISTORY/LORE

According to mythology, one day while the goddess of love, Venus, was sleeping, her son, Cupid, cut her fingernails with an arrowhead. The clippings fell into the sand, where they were transformed into stone; having come from part of an immortal being, the stone would never perish. In his 1550 work, *De Subtilitate*, the Italian mathematician, physician, astrologer, and philosopher Geronimo Cardano wrote of onyx being used in India to "cool the ardors of love."

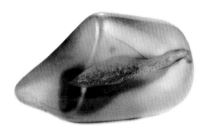

USES

Healing Uses: Onyx absorbs healing energies from the universe and then transfers them to those in need of healing. Specifically, this stone treats illnesses of the bones and blood, and it is also beneficial for the teeth and feet. Because of its connection to memory, onyx can be used to heal old injuries and physical trauma.

Magical Uses: Onyx is said to hold the memories of the wearer, making it useful for past-life work. It also offers protection during spiritual counseling, tarot card readings, channeling, or any other practice that invites psychic influences. Place onyx next to your bed to prevent nightmares or night terrors.

Feng Shui Uses: Onyx is an excellent stone for feng shui due to its stable, supportive energy and protective quality. Black onyx is associated with the northern area of a home or room as well as the Career/Path in Life sector. Keep onyx on your desk or wherever you perform work for mental focus and grounding.

Personal/Spiritual Growth: This stone recognizes and reconciles dualities within the self. It anchors those who tend toward erratic behavior and encourages self-control and steadfastness. Use onyx to overcome fears and anxiety, and for wisdom in decision-making.

Opal

ORIGINS

Opal is an iridescent mineral of hydrated silica. It is found in an array of colors and varieties, including blue, cherry, chrysopal (blue-green), fire (orange-red), green, and hyalite (clear, glassy). The most famous opal deposits are in Australia, where it is the national gemstone, but it is also found in the United States, Honduras, Brazil, and Slovakia. In 2008, NASA's Mars Reconnaissance Orbiter found opal on Mars, suggesting that liquid water remained on the planet's surface a billion years later than scientists had previously believed.

HISTORY/LORE

Australian Aboriginal legend describes the birth of opals: The Creator came down to Earth on a rainbow to bring the message of peace to all humans. On the spot where his foot touched, the stones became vibrant with color and began to sparkle, and this is how opal came to be. Opal plays a role in Sir Walter Scott's 1829 novel, *Anne of Geierstein*, in which he writes of "a superb opal, which, amid the changing lights peculiar to that gem, displayed internally a slight tinge of red like a spark of fire."

USES

Healing Uses: Opal cleanses the body, fights infections, and purifies the blood; cherry opal is especially helpful for blood disorders. Fire opal resonates with the abdomen and lower back, treating the intestines and kidneys. Green opal strengthens the immune system and battles colds and the flu. Hyalite, also called water opal, combats dehydration and enhances water retention.

Magical Uses: Opal is a delicate stone that supports cosmic consciousness and induces psychic and mystical visions. It reveals emotional information from the past, especially from past lives, and helps to incorporate that information into the present. Blue opal is particularly useful for this.

Feng Shui Uses: Generally speaking, opal uses water energy, the energy of stillness and purification, making it useful in the northern area of a home or room as well as the Career/Path in Life sector. Fire opal, on the other hand, uses fire energy, the energy of heat, action, and passion. Use this stone in the southern area of a home or room or in the Fame/Reputation sector.

Personal/Spiritual Growth: Opal is the birthstone for the month of October. This stone is wonderful for artists, as it stimulates creativity and originality. Chrysopal in particular opens the mind to new ideas and helps you to see the world with new eyes. Fire opal assists in business matters as well as situations of injustice or mistreatment. Green opal works wonders in relationships.

Rose Quartz

ORIGINS

Rose quartz is the pale pink to reddish pink variety of the mineral quartz, which is composed of silicon dioxide. The pink color is due to the presence of titanium, iron, manganese, or dumortierite in the stone. Rose quartz is found in the United States, Brazil, South Africa, Madagascar, India, and Japan.

HISTORY/LORE

The ancient Egyptians believed rose quartz could prevent aging. They used the powdered form in cosmetics to clear the complexion and stop wrinkles, and rose quartz facial masks intended for use in the afterlife have been found in ancient Egyptian tombs.

USES

Healing Uses: This stone's connection to the heart chakra makes it useful for strengthening the heart and circulatory system. Place rose quartz on the thymus (just above the heart) to treat chest and lung problems. The stone supports skin regeneration, soothes burns, and clears the complexion. It is also helpful for fertility, pregnancy, and birth issues, and it assists those with Parkinson's, Alzheimer's, or dementia.

Magical Uses: Rose quartz is often used in love rituals and spells, and as a divination tool when seeking guidance in matters of the heart. This stone helps to draw love toward you; in existing relationships it restores trust and encourages unconditional love. Use a rose quartz egg to grow love or enhance fertility.

Feng Shui Uses: Rose quartz uses subdued fire energy. Place rose quartz by your bed or in the Marriage/Relationships sector of your home to attract love. If this proves too powerful, use it with amethyst to calm things down.

Personal/Spiritual Growth: Rose quartz purifies and opens the heart on all levels, bringing deep inner healing and self-love. Wear the stone over the heart to increase these benefits. For meditation, hold a piece of rose quartz in your "receiving" hand (if you are right-handed, this is your left hand, and vice versa).

Ruby

ORIGINS

Ruby is a variety of the mineral corundum (aluminum oxide) that gets its red color from chromium impurities, which make the stone glow under ultraviolet light. The word *ruby* comes from the Latin *rubeus*, meaning "red." This very hard stone (9 on the Mohs scale) is found in many locations worldwide, including Kenya, Madagascar, India, and Myanmar (Burma).

HISTORY/LORE

Burma (now Myanmar) has been a major source of rubies since at least c.e. 600. Burmese warriors embedded rubies in their skin for protection during battle. Sanskrit medical texts prescribed rubies as a cure for health issues such as flatulence and biliousness. Hindu lore says that a ruby's light cannot be extinguished or hidden by clothing.

USES

Healing Uses: Ruby is a blood-related stone that stimulates the heart chakra. It detoxifies the blood and benefits the heart and circulatory system. It also alleviates pain associated with menstruation and regulates the menstrual flow. Ruby is helpful during pregnancy, particularly for older women. In fact, this stone is helpful for all issues related to reproduction, including infertility and impotence. Ruby also stimulates the adrenal glands, kidneys, and spleen.

Magical Uses: This stone balances the energies of the body and invigorates the mind. Use a ruby as a shield against psychic attack and vampirism of heart energy. Sleeping with a ruby under your pillow brings prophetic dreams and wards off nightmares. Dreaming of rubies indicates coming prosperity and good fortune—or unexpected guests.

Feng Shui Uses: Ruby uses fire energy, which brings warmth, light, and passion. Place this stone in the southern area of a space as well as in the Fame/Reputation sector of the home. This stone also brings abundance and assists in retaining wealth, making it useful in the Wealth/Prosperity sector.

Personal/Spiritual Growth: Ruby is the birthstone for the month of July. It encourages you to "follow your bliss" and embrace life on Earth. This stone is helpful for creative and intellectual pursuits, as it sharpens the mind, heightens awareness, and enhances concentration. Ruby is especially helpful for providing a boost of energy when you're feeling lethargic or unmotivated.

Sapphire

ORIGINS

Like ruby, sapphire is a variety of the mineral corundum (aluminum oxide). Although sapphire is most recognizable in the blue variety, which gets its color from traces of titanium and iron, this stone can be almost any color, including pink, yellow, and green, as well as colorless. Another variety is star sapphire, named for its inclusions of the mineral rutile, which appear as a six-rayed star image or "asterism." Sapphire is found in Madagascar, Sri Lanka, Myanmar (Burma), Australia, and other locations worldwide.

HISTORY/LORE

Sri Lanka has been an important source of gemstones for thousands of years and has produced some of the most famous sapphires in the world. The Star of India, exhibited at the American Museum of Natural History in New York City, is a 563-carat star sapphire that is around 2 billion years old. The Logan Sapphire, named after the person who donated it to Washington, DC's Smithsonian National Museum of Natural History in 1960, is a 423-carat sapphire about the size of an egg, mounted in a silver and gold brooch setting and surrounded by twenty brilliant-cut diamonds. For centuries, sapphires have been associated with royalty, a recent example of which is the sapphire engagement ring Prince Charles gave to Diana, now worn by Kate Middleton, Duchess of Cambridge.

USES

Healing Uses: Sapphire regulates the glands and treats blood disorders, and it also helps with sleep issues, such as insomnia. Green sapphire heals eye infections and improves eyesight. Blue sapphire connects with the throat chakra and heals the thyroid; wear it around the neck to increase these benefits. Yellow sapphire removes toxins from the body.

Magical Uses: Just as green sapphire enhances physical vision, it also improves inner vision and assists in dream recall. Wear blue sapphire at the throat to release frustration and facilitate self-expression. Star sapphire can enable a connection with extraterrestrial beings.

Feng Shui Uses: Each color of sapphire connects with a different kind of energy. Blue sapphire, for example, uses water energy, bringing regeneration and rebirth. For this reason, it should be placed in the northern area of a home or room, or in the Career/Path in Life sector. Yellow sapphire uses subdued fire energy and is most effective in the center of a home or room.

Personal/Spiritual Growth: Sapphire is the birthstone for the month of September. This stone brings peace of mind and serenity as well as spiritual power. Use sapphire for self-exploration and to increase confidence. Use it in meditation to illuminate spiritual truths.

Smoky Quartz

ORIGINS

Smoky quartz is a light to dark brown variety of quartz whose color and smoky appearance are caused by aluminum impurities and either natural or artificial irradiation of the stone. This stone is found in many locations in the world, including the United States, Brazil, Madagascar, and Australia. Cairngorm is a variety of smoky quartz crystal found in Scotland's Cairngorm Mountains.

HISTORY/LORE

Smoky quartz is the national gem of Scotland and has been important in that region of the world going back to the time of the Druids, whose earliest known records date back to the third century B.C.E. The stone was used to make sunglasses in China in the twelfth century.

USES

Healing Uses: Smoky quartz is very effective for pain relief, particularly headaches and muscle cramps. For this purpose, place a crystal on the painful spot with the point directed away from the body. This stone also regulates the fluids within the body and assists in the absorption of minerals. Because smoky quartz is irradiated, it is excellent for treating radiation-related issues and easing the negative effects of chemotherapy. However, be sure to select naturally formed stones rather than ones that have been artificially irradiated (artificially irradiated stones are usually darker in color, almost black and leaning toward opaque).

Magical Uses: Smoky quartz is a powerful stress reliever. To relieve stress, hold a stone in each hand and sit quietly for a few moments. Smoky quartz also neutralizes negative vibrations, guards against geopathic stress, and absorbs electromagnetic smog.

Feng Shui Uses: In feng shui, smoky quartz is a protective stone that is useful when placed near the front door of a home. It also uses wood energy, which makes it effective in the eastern and southeastern areas of a space as well as the Family/Foundation sector of the home.

Personal/Spiritual Growth: This stone has a strong connection to the root chakra, located at the base of the spine, which is our anchor in the natural world. Its grounding spiritual energy makes it excellent for meditation.

Tiger's Eye

ORIGINS

Tiger's eye is a type of quartz that is typically yellow-brown in color but can also be pink, red, or blue. It has a banded appearance and a silky sheen, due to its fibrous structure. Sources of tiger's eye include the United States, South Africa, India, and Australia. Tiger iron is a related stone, composed of tiger's eye, red jasper, and black hematite. Blue or blue-gray tiger's eye is called hawk's eye or falcon's eye.

HISTORY/LORE

For thousands of years, the various "eye" stones have been considered strong talismans with an "all-seeing" power. The ancient Egyptians used the stone for the eyes in statues of gods. Roman soldiers carried tiger's eye for courage and protection in battle.

USES

Healing Uses: Tiger's eye treats eye issues and enhances vision, and it also assists with neck and spinal problems. Red tiger's eye speeds up a slow metabolism. Hawk's eye aids the circulatory system, bowels, and legs.

Magical Uses: As a talisman, tiger's eye guards against curses. Placed on the third eye, this stone enhances psychic abilities and balances the lower chakras. Hawk's eye assists with clairvoyance.

Feng Shui Uses: Place tiger's eye near the front door or a large window to take advantage of its protective qualities. Hawk's eye attracts abundance when placed in the Wealth/Prosperity sector of the home.

Personal/Spiritual Growth: This stone helps in solving problems and resolving conflicts, and it also unblocks creativity. Place tiger's eye on the solar plexus/navel chakra for spiritual grounding. Red tiger's eye is a stimulating stone that battles lethargy and boosts motivation, helping you locate inner resources and accomplish your goals.

Topaz

ORIGINS

Topaz is a transparent silicate mineral of aluminum and fluorine that is quite hard (8 on the Mohs scale). It is most recognizable as a golden-yellow stone, but other varieties include brown, blue, pink, green, and colorless. Deposits of topaz have been found in the United States, Mexico, Pakistan, Sri Lanka, and Australia.

HISTORY/LORE

Up until the eleventh century the word *topaz*, which comes from the Greek *Topazios*, an island off the coast of Egypt in the Red Sea, was used to describe green gemstones. (Topazios, also known as St. John's Island, was an ancient source of the green gem peridot.) However, in his *Liber de lapidibus* (book of stones), Marbodus of Rennes (c. 1035–1123) stated that the color of topaz is yellow, and from then on this is how the stone was known. The twelfth-century German nun, writer, composer, philosopher, and mystic Saint Hildegard of Bingen (1098–1179) wrote about the healing powers of topaz soaked in wine.

USES

Healing Uses: Topaz is a wonderful healing stone. It aids digestion, stimulates the metabolism, and combats eating disorders such as anorexia and bulimia. Blue topaz assists with issues related to the throat and vocal cords.

Magical Uses: Topaz is very supportive in affirmation, manifestation, and visualization practices. Use topaz to make requests of the universe that you hope will manifest on the Earth plane. In the form of an amulet, topaz alleviates sadness and mood swings.

Feng Shui Uses: Topaz has a vibrant energy that replaces negativity with love and joy. This stone is most powerful in the center of a space or in the Health/Well-Being sector of the home.

Personal/Spiritual Growth: Along with citrine, topaz is a birthstone for the month of November. It is a mellow, empathetic stone that promotes truth and forgiveness. When placed on the throat or third eye it enhances communication abilities. Use blue topaz during meditation to access the higher self. Pink topaz helps to break old patterns.

Tourmaline

ORIGINS

Tourmaline is a crystalline silicate mineral containing aluminum, boron, and other elements. It is found in almost every color, including multicolored (elbaite) and pink-and-green "watermelon" varieties, but the most common type is iron-rich black tourmaline, also known as schorl. Tourmaline is found in the United States, Brazil, Africa, Afghanistan, and Sri Lanka.

HISTORY/LORE

When tourmaline was first mined, no distinction was made between it and other gemstones. Throughout history, "rubies" were often misidentified red tourmaline stones, and green tourmaline was often mistaken for emerald. Today, tourmaline is recognized and appreciated in its own right, and was popularized in the United States beginning in the late 1800s when Tiffany gemologist George F. Kunz praised the stones found in Maine and California.

USES

Healing Uses: The striations in a tourmaline crystal enhance energy flow, making this an excellent healing stone, particularly in wand form. Blue tourmaline is useful for identifying the underlying causes of a disease. Yellow tourmaline treats the digestive and cleansing organs of the body, including the stomach, liver, spleen, kidneys, and gallbladder. Red tourmaline heals the heart and blood vessels. Watermelon tourmaline helps to regenerate the nerves.

Magical Uses: Tourmaline is a shamanic stone that provides protection during rituals. It can be used for scrying or to indicate the direction in which a person should move. Blue tourmaline brings psychic awareness and facilitates visions. Brown tourmaline is an excellent grounding stone that also clears the aura. Wear black tourmaline to protect against electromagnetic smog, radiation, psychic attack, and spells.

Feng Shui Uses: Black tourmaline uses water energy and is the best variety of this stone for feng shui. It is most beneficial when placed in the northern area of a space or the Career/Path in Life sector of the home.

Personal/Spiritual Growth: Watermelon tourmaline activates the heart chakra, providing a link to the higher self and promoting love, tenderness, and friendship. Green tourmaline inspires creativity. Black tourmaline clears negative thoughts and fosters a laid-back, positive attitude, regardless of the circumstances.

Turquoise

ORIGINS

Turquoise is an opaque mineral that is found in various shades of blue and green, due to the copper in its composition. The word *turquoise* comes from the Old French *turqueise*, meaning "Turkish." The stone is found in the United States, Mexico, France, Egypt, the Middle East, Russia, Peru, China, and Tibet.

HISTORY/LORE

This stone gets its name from the incorrect belief that it came from Turkey. Though turquoise was traded in Turkey, it was imported from other places, mainly Iran and the Sinai Peninsula. The ancient Egyptians, Sumerians, and Aztecs prized turquoise, and some Native American tribes consider turquoise a sacred stone that connects earth and heaven.

USES

Healing Uses: Turquoise calms the emotions and promotes feelings of peace and well-being. It can help to balance mood swings, reduce stress, and ease depression. Its purifying properties can aid detoxification and protect against environmental pollution. Turquoise aligns with the throat and heart chakras; therefore, wearing it as a necklace can enhance communication, soothe throat complaints, and lessen emotional suffering.

Magical Uses: A popular stone for healing spells, turquoise can be worn or carried to encourage emotional and physical well-being. As an amulet, it offers protection against physical, psychic, and environmental harm. As a talisman, it brings good fortune and abundance.

Feng Shui Uses: Place a piece of turquoise in the Wealth/Prosperity sector of your home or business to attract fortune. Put it in the Marriage/Relationships sector to encourage harmony and happiness in a romantic partnership. In the Health/Well-Being sector, it draws healing energy and restores energetic balance.

Personal/Spiritual Growth: Meditate with turquoise to improve your connection with the spiritual realm. As it strengthens the emotions, turquoise helps you gain confidence and release self-limiting behaviors. It can also reduce feelings of loneliness and isolation, enabling you to realize a deeper link with "all that is."

2

THE POWER OF HERBS:
Herbs and Spices

Behold the power of plants! All of the herbs and spices in this chapter come from the ground and have myriad uses for the mind and body. Although Western society has largely stopped using plants for medicinal purposes, they can sometimes be more effective, less expensive, and safer than their pharmaceutical counterparts.

Depending on the plant, you can use the leaves, flowers, berries, and/or roots in fresh, dried, or powdered form. Some of these items will already be in your spice cabinet or garden; others you can easily obtain from the grocery or health food store. You may be surprised to learn that some of these herbs have uses beyond the ones you already know. For example, you may be accustomed to including bay leaves in your homemade tomato sauce, but have you ever used the leaves to make a soothing digestive tea? Did you know that dandelions are not only edible but also good for you? And here's a fun one: In addition to being a delicious culinary herb, sage is also used in a practice called "saging" to remove negative energy from a space. How cool is that?

Generally speaking, herbs are natural and healthy and safe, but there are a few exceptions. If you are taking any prescription medications, be sure to consult your doctor before experimenting with herbal remedies, as this could result in negative interactions. Also, some herbs, such as valerian, can be habit-forming if taken in large quantities or for prolonged periods of time. It is recommended that you start small when trying herbal remedies and pay attention to your body's responses. If something doesn't work for you, try something else. There are plenty of herbs out there!

Angelica

ORIGINS

Angelica is an herb in the parsley family. The plant is tall with large compound umbels of white or greenish flowers. The stems can be candied and eaten, and the roots can be used for flavoring liqueurs. Angelica is native to temperate and subarctic regions of the Northern Hemisphere, including Norway, Lithuania, and Russia. *Angelica* comes from the Greek *angelos*, meaning "messenger."

HISTORY/LORE

According to legend, an angel came to a monk in a dream to reveal a plant that would cure the plague (hence the name). Angelica is one of the main ingredients in Carmelite water, a lemon balm–based tonic created by Carmelite monks in the 1600s to cure headaches, promote relaxation, and protect the drinker against poisons and spells. A related herb called Chinese angelica, or dong quai, has been used in Chinese medicine for thousands of years.

USES

Healing Uses: Angelica is used to cure fevers, colds, and coughs, and it is particularly effective as an expectorant to clear chest congestion. It is also helpful for bringing on menstruation and relieving bloating or cramps; pregnant women should not use angelica, as it could cause a miscarriage. Angelica contains compounds that act like calcium channel blockers, which are used to treat conditions such as high blood pressure, migraines, and Raynaud's disease.

Magical Uses: Angelica protects against negative energy and attracts positive energy. Grow angelica in the garden to protect the home. Sprinkle dried angelica leaves in the four corners of the home to ward off evil spirits. Burn dried angelica leaves for exorcism. Add angelica to bathwater to remove curses, hexes, or spells. Use angelica root in potpourri.

Personal/Spiritual Growth: Angelica relaxes the mind and stimulates the imagination. It offers strength and balance and is especially helpful during difficult times when you feel cut off from your inner self. As an essential oil, angelica has a revitalizing effect, making it useful for when you're going through a sluggish period.

Arnica

ORIGINS

Arnica is a perennial herb in the Asteraceae or Compositae family, which also includes asters, daisies, and sunflowers. The *Arnica montana* species has yellow or orange flowers, and the flowers and roots are dried and used for medicinal and other purposes. *Arnica montana* is native to Europe and Siberia, but other species in the Arnica genus also grow in North America, particularly in mountainous regions.

HISTORY/LORE

Arnica has several nicknames, including wolf's bane (which it confusingly shares with aconite) and mountain tobacco. Though it has a long history of medicinal use in many cultures, the use of arnica is especially touted in Germany. The German writer Johann Wolfgang von Goethe (1749–1832), who suffered from angina, credited arnica with saving his life.

USES

Healing Uses: Dried arnica flowers placed in bathwater will ease general aches and pains. Arnica oil relieves muscle soreness, swelling, and inflammation. Arnica should not be placed directly on an open wound; instead, place a compress of dried flowers and roots over a bandaged wound for pain relief and to aid the healing process. This herb should be taken internally only under the supervision of a certified herbalist, as it can cause gastrointestinal distress and other negative reactions.

Magical Uses: Arnica flowers increase psychic powers. This herb is also associated with the harvest and can be used in rituals to ensure the fertility of crops. For protection, add the dried flowers to boiling water to make a tea, and then sprinkle the liquid around the door and window frames of the home.

Personal/Spiritual Growth: Following a traumatic experience, lots of negative and painful emotions may be present. If not dealt with, these emotions can manifest physically as illnesses and other conditions. Meditate with arnica essence to release pent-up pain from past trauma, gain wisdom, and move forward in a balanced, harmonized way. Arnica essential oil can be used in aromatherapy to promote positivity and gratitude.

Basil

ORIGINS

Basil (*Ocimum basilicum*) is an aromatic annual herb in the mint family that is native to Africa and Asia. The word *basil* comes from the Greek *basilikos*, meaning "royal." A variant called holy basil, or *tulsi*, is native to India and plays an important role in the Hindu religion.

HISTORY/LORE

In ancient Greece, basil was associated with grief and mourning. In the sixteenth century in Europe it was believed that scorpions were attracted to basil and that a basil sprig left under a pot containing a basil plant would turn into a scorpion. A French doctor once wrote that smelling basil would cause a scorpion to grow in the brain.

USES

Healing Uses: As a tea, basil eases stomach pain, cramps, indigestion, and constipation, and it also stimulates lactation in nursing mothers. The French herbalist Maurice Mességué recommends basil for restlessness and migraines. The herb also has antibacterial and antifungal properties (use the oil for best results in these cases).

Magical Uses: Basil is useful in love spells and love divination. To divine the future of a romantic relationship, place two basil leaves on a live coal. If they remain where you placed them and turn to ash quickly, the relationship will be harmonious. If they crackle and move, the relationship will be rocky. Burn basil to cleanse a home of negativity. Given as a gift, basil brings good luck to a new home.

Personal/Spiritual Growth: Basil brings courage and strength to those who are fearful and helps to clear clouded judgment. It also eases anxiety and improves communication. Use holy basil for prayer and meditation or to enhance memory. Place basil in bathwater to get over an old love or to invite new love in. See the basil entry in Chapter 4 to learn about the benefits of basil essential oil.

Bay Laurel

ORIGINS

Bay laurel (*Laurus nobilis*) is an aromatic evergreen tree, native to the Mediterranean region, that produces the bay leaf commonly used in cooking. The leaves can be used fresh or dried (fresh is stronger) but should be removed before serving because they are difficult to digest. A bay leaf placed in a container of rice or flour is thought to deter pests.

HISTORY/LORE

In ancient times, a wreath of laurel was given as a sign of honor or victory (hence the term *laureate*). To "rest on one's laurels" is to rely on past successes for future fame or recognition. The Greek god Apollo is always depicted wearing a laurel wreath on his head to represent his love for the nymph Daphne, whose father turned her into a laurel tree to protect her from Apollo's advances.

USES

Healing Uses: Bay laurel oil can be used with massage to soothe muscle aches and pains. As a salve, bay laurel soothes bruises, itching, and minor skin irritations. A tea made of the leaves and berries aids digestion and has a calming effect. Adding bay laurel to bathwater treats vaginal infections and assists with healing after childbirth. Burn bay leaves in a sick room to purify the space following an illness.

Magical Uses: Bay laurel is very effective in purification rituals, especially smudging. Mixed with sandalwood, it is useful for breaking curses. Use bay laurel during meditation for clairvoyance. Place bay laurel in your pillowcase to encourage sound sleep and induce prophetic dreams.

Personal/Spiritual Growth: Bay laurel heightens intuition, awareness, and perception. Burn a candle dressed with bay laurel oil to bring about personal change. Write a wish or desire on a bay leaf and then burn it to make it come true. Use bay laurel essential oil to boost confidence, encourage inspiration, and promote creativity.

Black Cohosh

ORIGINS

Black cohosh (*Actaea racemosa*) is a plant in the buttercup (Ranunculaceae) family with tall, white flowering racemes (flower stalks). A perennial plant, it is native to North America and typically grows in woodland areas. Other names for black cohosh include black snakeroot, due to its history as a snakebite remedy, and black bugbane, because it is known to repel insects. A related plant, blue cohosh, has similar attributes.

HISTORY/LORE

The Native Americans have used black cohosh for centuries to treat a number of conditions, including gynecological issues, kidney problems, headaches, and depression. In nineteenth-century America, the plant was used as a home remedy for rheumatism and fever, as a diuretic, and to bring on menstruation.

USES

Healing Uses: Black cohosh, which contains a compound thought to have estrogenic activity, is used to treat hot flashes, night sweats, vaginal dryness, and other symptoms of menopause. For this reason, it is often prescribed as an alternative to estrogen replacement therapy (also called hormone replacement therapy). It also eases premenstrual tension and cramps. Black cohosh is occasionally used to treat skin conditions such as acne and for healing following wart or mole removal. It can also be used to treat rheumatism, lung conditions, and neurological issues.

Magical Uses: Black cohosh is a protective plant. Sprinkle it around the home, burn as incense, or use the tea as a floor wash to keep evil and negative influences at bay. Carry black cohosh in your pocket for courage, faith, and determination. Used in a sachet, black cohosh preserves and maintains existing love or invites new love into your life.

Personal/Spiritual Growth: Black cohosh assists with transformation. Its black roots represent darkness in the past, and its white flowers are the promise of a bright future. Use this herb to release yourself from old attachments and move confidently forward into a new phase of your life. Added to bathwater, it brings courage.

Black Pepper

ORIGINS

This pungent spice comes from the pepper plant (*Piper nigrum*), which is native to south India but also grows in other parts of the world, particularly tropical regions. The small, unripe fruits of this plant are dried (peppercorns) and ground to make the spice found in household peppershakers.

HISTORY/LORE

Dubbed "black gold," black pepper has been used in India for thousands of years. The ancient Egyptians also used this spice. The Egyptian pharaoh Ramesses II (1301–1213 B.C.E.) was entombed with black peppercorns in his nostrils, most likely for preservation and to maintain the shape of his nose. His mummy is now on display at the Egyptian Museum in Cairo.

USES

Healing Uses: Black pepper has powerful digestive properties. The aroma and spicy flavor of black pepper trigger the stomach to produce hydrochloric acid, which is needed to digest protein, and they also stimulate the pancreas to produce important digestive enzymes. Piperine, the alkaloid that makes black pepper so pungent, has antioxidant qualities. In Western herbalism, black pepper is used in cold and flu remedies. In Ayurvedic medicine, black pepper is mixed with honey to treat respiratory congestion.

Magical Uses: Black pepper banishes negativity and protects against evil, and can also be used in exorcisms. It is useful for cleansing a previously occupied home for a new owner. Carry black pepper with you to banish feelings of jealousy and to protect yourself from the jealousy of others.

Personal/Spiritual Growth: Black pepper is wonderful for relieving anxiety and stress. It encourages you to release those negative influences and find your inner source of power. Black pepper helps you "digest" unhealthy feelings toward yourself and others, while providing the courage and stamina needed to get through the process and move forward. Black pepper essential oil has various health benefits, such as supporting digestion and soothing sore muscles, and it can also be used in aromatherapy to boost energy.

Calendula

ORIGINS

Calendula (*Calendula officinalis*), more commonly known as marigold, is a flowering plant native to the Mediterranean region. The word *calendula* comes from the Latin *kalendae*, meaning "calends," the first day of the month in the ancient Roman calendar. The more common name, marigold, is a reference to the Virgin Mary.

HISTORY/LORE

According to legend, a Greek maiden named Caltha fell in love with Apollo, the sun god. Consumed by her love, she waited in the fields all night, hoping to catch first sight of him in the morning. Eventually she wasted away and died, and a marigold, bright yellow like the sun, appeared in the place where she had stood. In India, marigolds are sacred to the goddess Mahadevi and are worn as garlands at the festival honoring her.

USES

Healing Uses: Place a compress saturated with warm calendula tea on wounds and skin inflammations, including rashes and insect bites. You can also use calendula essential oil for this purpose, as it has a gentle, cooling effect. Taken internally, calendula cleanses the lymph system and aids in healing ulcers. This plant also relieves pain associated with menstruation. One way to enjoy the herb's health benefits is to use it as a substitute for saffron in dishes such as yellow rice.

Magical Uses: Wreaths of marigold hung over a doorway are said to keep evil and negativity from entering a home. Sprinkle marigold petals on the floor under the bed to bring prophetic dreams. Burn marigold petals as incense for divination. Adding marigold petals to bathwater assists with career aspirations.

Personal/Spiritual Growth: Calendula projects a warm, healing light and offers comfort to those who are fearful, nervous, or recovering from the shock of a trauma. It encourages understanding and compassion and tempers anger and rash behavior. In meditation, calendula brings clarity.

Cayenne

ORIGINS

Cayenne pepper is a hot chili pepper that is commonly used in its dried or powdered form to flavor dishes. It is a member of the genus *Capsicum*, which also includes bell peppers, jalapeños, and others. This pepper is native to the Americas and gets its name from the capital city of French Guiana.

HISTORY/LORE

Records show that cayenne pepper was in use in Central and South America as early as 8000 B.C.E. Christopher Columbus introduced the pepper to Europe in the late fifteenth century. The American herbalist and botanist Samuel Thompson (1769–1843) created an alternative system of medicine that included cayenne pepper in many of its remedies to restore the body's inner heat.

USES

Healing Uses: Cayenne pepper is a go-to cure for headaches, colds, and the flu. It is also used to treat digestive and intestinal problems, including ulcers. Cayenne boosts the metabolism and circulation and benefits the heart. It is also used to lower blood pressure. Used as a counterirritant it soothes such conditions as rheumatism and arthritis. Cayenne cleanses the body of toxins and poisons and supports the immune system.

Magical Uses: Cayenne pepper is useful for vision quests. It also enhances the power of other herbs and speeds up the effects of spells. Scatter cayenne pepper around your house to break bad spells or hexes. Used in love spells, cayenne adds "spice" to an existing romance or brings new love. Include cayenne in purification rituals to clear away negative influences.

Personal/Spiritual Growth: Cayenne pepper energizes the spirit by energizing the body. This process brings heightened spiritual awareness of the invisible world. Cayenne can also be used to bring spice and heat to romantic relationships, or to cope with the pain of separation or divorce. This spice balances the heart chakra.

Chamomile

ORIGINS

Native to Europe and the Mediterranean, chamomile is an aromatic perennial herb in the Asteraceae family. The most commonly used variety is German chamomile (*Matricaria recutita* or *Matricaria chamomilla*). The flowers of the chamomile plant are its most useful part; with white petals and yellow centers, they bear a strong resemblance to daisies. The word *chamomile* comes from the Greek *khamaimelon: khamai*, meaning "on the ground," and *melon*, meaning "apple."

HISTORY/LORE

Chamomile was used for medicinal purposes in the ancient Egyptian, Greek, and Roman civilizations. Greek physicians prescribed it for fevers and female issues. In her 1911 book, *The Herb Garden*, Frances A. Bardwell praises chamomile for the positive effect it has on other plants. Roman chamomile (*Chamaemelum nobile*) is used to flavor Spanish sherry.

USES

Healing Uses: Chamomile is a calming herb that reduces stress. Drink chamomile tea to ease stomach discomfort and aid digestion, or to relax in the evening and ensure a good night's sleep. For fevers, colds, and the flu, combine dried chamomile flowers with boiling water and inhale the steam for up to 10 minutes. Chamomile tea can also be applied externally, to treat burns, skin infections, and hemorrhoids. Chamomile essential oil soothes sore muscles following exercise.

Magical Uses: Because chamomile creates abundance, it is especially useful in money spells. To remove a curse or a hex, steep chamomile in warm water and then sprinkle with basil. Spread dried chamomile flowers around the home to ward off negative influences and provide protection. Add chamomile to bathwater to attract love.

Personal/Spiritual Growth: Chamomile has a soothing, sedating effect that is helpful when you are experiencing anxiety, going through a difficult time, or recovering from a traumatic experience. When your mind won't shut off, this herb has a quieting effect that can bring calm and comfort. Use chamomile as incense during meditation to feel centered and peaceful.

Cinnamon

ORIGINS

Cinnamon is the dried inner bark of certain tropical Asian trees of the genus *Cinnamomum*. It is most commonly used in stick or powdered form to add flavor to foods and beverages, but it also has various medicinal and magical uses. Sri Lanka is a major source of cinnamon, as are Indonesia and China.

HISTORY/LORE

Cinnamon has been used in Chinese medicine for over 4,000 years. In ancient Egypt, it was not only consumed; it was also used in embalming practices. Legend has it that the Roman emperor Nero (37–68) burned all the cinnamon he could find on the funeral pyre of his second wife, Poppaea Sabina, to punish himself for his role in her death. Cinnamon is mentioned in the Bible as an ingredient in anointing oil.

USES

Healing Uses: Cinnamon relieves stomach discomfort, including morning sickness and motion sickness, and can be used to treat digestive problems such as gas, diarrhea, and vomiting. Cinnamon is also useful for treating sore throats, coughs, colds, headaches, and the flu. In Ayurvedic medicine, cinnamon is used as a remedy for diabetes.

Magical Uses: Cinnamon relates to the element of fire and is therefore extra powerful when burned. Burn cinnamon as incense to bring love or ignite passion. Use cinnamon in love or sex spells, or to enhance psychic powers. Hang a bundle of cinnamon sticks above the doorway to protect the home from negative influences.

Personal/Spiritual Growth: Cinnamon is a powerful healer, both physically and emotionally. It is the perfect spice for when you are feeling down or depressed. Use it in a sachet to raise protective and spiritual vibrations. Cinnamon brings good fortune in matters of money and business as well as games of chance. See the cinnamon entry in Chapter 4 to learn about the benefits of cinnamon essential oil.

Clove

ORIGINS

Clove is an evergreen tree (*Syzygium aromaticum*) native to the Maluku Islands, an archipelago within Indonesia also called the "Spice Islands." The flower bud of this tree is used in its dried form, either whole or ground—you may have one or both in your spice cabinet. The word *clove* comes from the Latin *clavus*, meaning "nail." Take a look at a clove and you'll see why!

HISTORY/LORE

Archaeologists found cloves in a vessel in Syria that dates back to 1721 B.C.E. The ancient Chinese chewed cloves to freshen their breath. Experts believe the world's oldest clove tree, estimated to be between 350 and 400 years old, is one called Afo, located on the island of Ternate. In Indonesia, clove cigarettes, called *kreteks*, are extremely popular.

USES

Healing Uses: Cloves can be used to treat toothaches, gum problems, and bad breath. Add cloves to tea to help clear up a respiratory infection. Eugenol, a natural antiseptic found in cloves, makes this spice useful for treating acne. Cloves are packed with antioxidants and are also effective for treating heartburn, indigestion, and nausea. Clove is often used as a natural insect repellent. Use clove-infused water in a warm compress to soothe aching eyes.

Magical Uses: Clove is a very protective spice. It can be used to ward off negative forces, stop harmful gossip, and keep good friends close. Burn cloves to cleanse and purify a space. Infuse wine or apple cider with cloves to create a delicious aphrodisiac. Wear cloves in an amulet to stimulate the memory.

Personal/Spiritual Growth: Clove dispels negativity and cleanses the aura. It rejuvenates physical and mental energy and fosters courage and inner strength. It can also be used for protection or to attract love. See the clove entry in Chapter 4 to learn about the benefits of clove essential oil.

Comfrey

ORIGINS

The term *comfrey* is used to describe various perennial herbs of the genus *Symphytum*. It comes from the Latin *confervere*, meaning "to boil together." (The origin of the word *fervent* is also evident here—*fervere* meaning "to boil.") The most common variety is Russian comfrey, which has pink or purple flowers. Comfrey grows well in most temperate regions, including North America, Europe, western Asia, and Australia.

HISTORY/LORE

The ancient Greek physician, pharmacologist, and botanist Pedanius Dioscorides (c. 40–90) included comfrey in his writings about herbal medicine. Legend has it that comfrey was one of the herbs growing in the Garden of Eden. In the New World, the settlers relied on comfrey to treat various illnesses and conditions. It was once believed that adding comfrey to bathwater could heal the hymen and restore a woman's virginity.

THE POWER OF HERBS

USES

Healing Uses: Comfrey is excellent for treating wounds, particularly those that are dirty or have become infected (use a compress soaked with warm comfrey tea for this). Its ability to heal broken bones earned it the nickname "knitbone," and it also assists with strains, sprains, and torn ligaments. As a poultice, it relieves bruises and soreness. This herb also assists with coughs and other lung-related issues.

Magical Uses: Comfrey is used in rituals to protect travelers; place it in your luggage to prevent your bags from being stolen. Wrap your money in a comfrey leaf for several days before any gambling endeavors to increase your chances of winning. Burn comfrey to let go of an unhealthy relationship. Use comfrey in healing and love spells, or include in love sachets.

Personal/Spiritual Growth: Comfrey is a grounding herb that provides a sense of structure when things feel chaotic. It soothes emotional pain and provides comfort during difficult times. Use comfrey to enforce boundaries, both physical and spiritual. Add this herb to bathwater for spiritual cleansing.

Dandelion

ORIGINS

Known to most people as a common weed, dandelion (*Taraxacum officinale*) is a perennial plant with bright yellow flowers that is found worldwide. The leaves, flowers, and roots are all used for various medicinal and culinary purposes. The yellow flower heads mature and turn into feathery, white seed heads that then disperse in the wind, spreading the seeds far and wide. The word *dandelion* comes from the Latin *dens leonis*, meaning "lion's tooth."

HISTORY/LORE

Because dandelion flowers open early in the morning and close in the evening, the dandelion is sometimes called the shepherd's clock. It is said that if the seeds fly off a dandelion seed head when there is no wind it means rain is coming.

USES

Healing Uses: Dandelion is often used as a diuretic and to purify the cleansing organs. It contains taraxacin and choline, which stimulate liver cell metabolism. It is also rich in vitamins A, B-complex, C, and E, as well as calcium. A tea made from dandelion roots is useful as a general health tonic. Rub the milky juice of the dandelion stem on warts.

Magical Uses: Blow on the white puffball of a dandelion seed head to check in with a relationship: If one seed remains after blowing on the seed head three times, it means your sweetheart is thinking of you. Then whisper a message to the flower and blow it in the direction of your loved one. Drinking a tea of dandelion flowers increases psychic abilities. Pour boiling water over dandelion root for divination. Include dandelion in a dream pillow to ward off nightmares.

Personal/Spiritual Growth: Dandelion stimulates the solar plexus chakra, the core of who we are. It helps to focus scattered emotions and strengthen the sense of self. This plant encourages those who are fearful of change to take action and move forward in life. Dandelions are excellent for making wishes. Make your wish, and then blow on the seed head to release your wish with the seeds.

Echinacea

ORIGINS

Echinacea is a genus that includes several flowering plants in the daisy family. These coneflowers, as they're called, have pink or purple petals and are native to North America. The word *echinacea* comes from the Latin *echinus*, meaning "sea urchin"—a reference to the plant's bristly seed head.

HISTORY/LORE

The Plains Native Americans used echinacea root as a painkiller and to treat colds, sore throats, wounds, and snakebites. The purple coneflower is still harvested by the Lakota people for medicinal uses. Echinacea was very popular in the United States in the eighteenth and nineteenth centuries, but its use declined after the introduction of antibiotics.

USES

Healing Uses: Echinacea raises white blood cell count, stimulates the immune system, and has anti-carcinogenic, antibiotic, and anti-inflammatory properties. Chew on the root or drink as tea to fight infection or prevent colds and flu—or to decrease their duration if they have already taken hold. To relieve skin inflammation, burns, or insect bites, saturate a compress in echinacea tea and place on the affected area. Echinacea essential oil is very useful with massage. Rub it on the temples and the back of the neck to relieve tension in the head, neck, and shoulders.

Magical Uses: Echinacea grown around the house brings prosperity and protects the family from suffering. It can also be used as an offering to the spirits or to enhance the power of spells. Burn echinacea as incense in cleansing rituals, making sure to let the smoke waft freely throughout the space.

Personal/Spiritual Growth: Many spiritual and physical ailments are a result of denying who you really are. Echinacea awakens the true inner self and assists in integrating that self with the outside world. This plant is also useful during major transitions, giving you strength and stamina in times of change. Echinacea also brings the mind and body into balance, creating a sense of inner harmony.

Evening Primrose

ORIGINS

Evening primrose is a flowering plant of the Onagraceae family, which is native to the Americas. Its cup-shaped yellow flowers have four petals each and open in the evening (hence the name). The young roots and shoots can be eaten like a vegetable, and the whole plant can be used for medicinal and other purposes.

HISTORY/LORE

Many Native American tribes, including the Cherokee, Iroquois, and Ojibwa, used evening primrose for various rituals and remedies. They used it as a poultice to treat bruises, as a salve to relieve skin irritations, and as a tea for weight loss. Evening primrose root was also heated and applied to hemorrhoids to relieve pain and reduce swelling. The Shakers, a religious sect founded in England in the eighteenth century, used evening primrose in many of their natural remedies, including poultices for wounds and teas for upset stomach.

USES

Healing Uses: Evening primrose is high in essential fatty acids that are necessary for good health. Women can take evening primrose oil as a nutritional supplement to ease symptoms of PMS or to boost fertility. The oil can also be used to treat skin issues such as eczema and rosacea by applying it to the affected area. A tea made from the leaves, stems, and roots, applied externally, is nourishing for the skin.

Magical Uses: Because it blooms at night, evening primrose is great for use in moon ceremonies. Add evening primrose to bathwater to enhance inner beauty or use it in a spell for good luck in your career. It can also be used to attract faeries.

Personal/Spiritual Growth: As an evening bloomer, this flower shines its own light in the dark and encourages you to do the same. Evening primrose stimulates the solar plexus and heart chakras, allowing you to open yourself up to love without fear of betrayal or rejection. It also enhances creativity.

Fennel

ORIGINS

Fennel (*Foeniculum vulgare*) is a plant in the parsley and carrot family with small yellow flowers grouped in umbels. Native to the Mediterranean region, this herb is very flavorful and aromatic. All parts of the plant, including the seeds, can be eaten, although the stalks are tough and not used as often. The white bulb and green fronds have a slightly sweet anise flavor.

HISTORY/LORE

Fennel has been used as a medicinal and culinary herb for thousands of years. In ancient Greece, athletes ate the seeds as a health food and to control their weight. The Romans had numerous medicinal uses for fennel, including the treatment of eye ailments. In the twelfth century, the German nun, writer, composer, philosopher, and mystic Saint Hildegard of Bingen (1098–1179) noted fennel's eye-healing properties.

USES

Healing Uses: As a tea, fennel treats dizziness, coughs, and headaches. It can also be used as an expectorant to clear congestion. Fennel supports digestion and relieves abdominal cramps and flatulence, and it also increases milk flow in nursing mothers. The essential oil is especially useful during menstruation. Chewing fennel seeds freshens the breath. For animals, use fennel to get rid of a flea infestation by crushing the seeds and either sprinkling them around the home or rubbing them into the animal's coat.

Magical Uses: Burn fennel as incense to purify a space or to prevent curses. Hang fennel over a doorway with Saint John's wort to ward off evil spirits. Include fennel in sachets to remove negativity. Use fennel essential oil for protection spells and rituals. It can also be used in love spells and fertility rituals, as it is thought to boost sexual energy and increase fertility.

Personal/Spiritual Growth: Fennel is associated with strength, courage, and protection, and it is particularly helpful in the face of danger. It improves relationships, assists in establishing boundaries, and helps others trust in your word. Fennel essential oil is excellent for grounding during meditation and other spiritual practices.

Garlic

ORIGINS

Native to central Asia, garlic (*Allium sativum*) is an onion-like plant with a bulb that separates into cloves. It has a strong flavor and odor; hence the nickname "stinking rose." Although it grows worldwide, China is the largest producer of garlic. The word *garlic* comes from the Old English *garleac*: *gar*, meaning spear, and *leac*, meaning "leek."

HISTORY/LORE

The Romans used garlic to fend off evil spirits, and Greek soldiers carried it to prevent misfortune. In Romania, it was common practice to place garlic cloves in the mouths of the corpses of those thought to be vampires. Many traits of vampires, including their aversion to garlic, are also symptoms of a condition called porphyria, characterized by large amounts of porphyrins in the blood and urine. (Garlic exacerbates the disease.)

USES

Healing Uses: Garlic is used to improve digestion and ease stomach cramps. It also cleanses the blood, increases circulation, and prevents heart attacks and strokes. Garlic bolsters the immune system and protects against and fights off illness, including the common cold and the flu. Garlic contains compounds that break down carcinogenic chemicals. Ingesting too much garlic can cause stomach inflammation, ulcers, and anemia.

Magical Uses: Garlic is a very protective plant. It guards against negativity, evil, and the envy of others. It can also be used for exorcisms or to break curses. Carry a garlic clove with you when traveling over water to prevent drowning. Hang braided garlic above doorways to discourage unwanted visitors. Use in spells to drive away an unwanted lover.

Personal/Spiritual Growth: Garlic assists with spiritual healing by removing negative energy and strengthening your inner self. It also fortifies willpower and helps you keep your sights on your goals, even when faced with obstacles. Additionally, garlic fights envy and jealousy in oneself and others.

Ginger

ORIGINS

Ginger (*Zingiber officinale*) is a tropical Southeast Asian plant with yellowish-green flowers and a pungent aromatic root. Gingerroot, as it is also called, is used either fresh or dried for both medicinal and culinary purposes. Because of its spicy flavor, this root is associated with energy and vigor. "Ginger" is also slang for a person who has red hair.

HISTORY/LORE

Ginger has been featured in ancient Chinese medicine for thousands of years. It was highly valued by the ancient Romans, but its use decreased dramatically after the fall of the Roman Empire. It was picked up again in Europe and in the sixteenth century was introduced to Africa and the Caribbean. Jamaican ginger was the first spice to be grown in the New World and exported back to Europe.

USES

Healing Uses: Ginger has long been known as a stomach settler. It relieves nausea and vomiting associated with migraines, morning sickness, and motion sickness, and it is also helpful to those recovering from surgery or undergoing chemotherapy. Ginger treats the inflammation associated with arthritis, not only masking the pain but also fostering changes in the joints. Ginger is also a microbial herb that fights infectious illness. Incorporating ginger into recipes and drinking it as a tea are the easiest ways to partake of its benefits.

Magical Uses: Ginger adds fire to any magical activity. It speeds up the process of spells and helps plans develop more quickly. It can also be used in spells to "spice up" an existing relationship. As an amulet, ginger enhances health and protection. Burn powdered ginger to break curses.

Personal/Spiritual Growth: Ginger's digestive qualities extend into the spiritual realm. It helps you process ideas and emotions and provides the motivation needed to bring them into the physical realm. As an essential oil, ginger can bring energy and vitality. It is also a powerful aphrodisiac, corresponding to the sacral chakra, which governs pleasure.

Ginseng

ORIGINS

Ginseng encompasses several species of plants of the genus *Panax* with forked roots and small greenish flowers grouped in umbels. The major varieties of ginseng include Asian (*Panax ginseng*) and American (*Panax quinquefolius*). Another major variety, Siberian ginseng (*Eleutherococcus senticosus*), is in the same family as the first two but of a different genus. The word *ginseng* comes from the Mandarin *renshen*: *ren*, meaning "person," and *shen*, meaning "root"— most likely due to the forked root shape's resemblance to human legs.

HISTORY/LORE

Ginseng has been used in China for 5,000 years. Because Chinese emperors treasured the plant, it became highly valued and in demand. The Native Americans are responsible for ginseng's cultivation in North America. The Cherokee, Iroquois, and other tribes used ginseng as a remedy for various ailments and for general life enhancement.

USES

Healing Uses: Ginseng is considered a panacea—a cure-all. It is an adaptogen, a natural substance that helps the body adapt to stress, and it also lowers blood sugar levels. Ginseng is associated with stimulation and virility and is a common remedy for impotence. Those taking heart medications such as blood thinners should not take ginseng, as it could result in a negative interaction.

Magical Uses: Ginseng is a powerful love herb. It generates passion and lust, especially when drunk as a tea. Burn ginseng root or powder as incense to repel negativity, drive away evil, and break hexes or curses. Carry ginseng root with you to attract love or money. As an amulet, it brings good fortune, prosperity, longevity, and fertility.

Personal/Spiritual Growth: Ginseng boosts both mental and physical energy levels, which can then be used to harness internal power. It reduces psychological stress and sharpens mental powers. Ginseng also aids in visualization fulfillment. Take ginseng before meditation for enhanced clarity and a sense of calm.

Hyssop

ORIGINS

Hyssop (*Hyssopus officinalis*) is a plant in the mint family with spikes of blue or purple flowers and aromatic leaves. The hyssop plant is of Eurasian origin but also grows in North America. Both the leaves and flowers of the hyssop plant are used for medicinal and other purposes, and hyssop oil is used as a flavoring and a fragrance. Beekeepers love hyssop, as it produces a rich, aromatic honey.

HISTORY/LORE

Though it is not identified by name, it is believed that hyssop is one of the aromatic herbs mentioned in the Bible as a purification substance, particularly to cleanse the sinful. The herbs were dipped in water or vinegar and then waved like a wand over the afflicted persons, often lepers.

USES

Healing Uses: Hyssop tea is effective as an expectorant or cough suppressant, and it can also be used to treat digestive and intestinal problems, including gas and loss of appetite. Adding hyssop to bathwater eases the pain associated with rheumatoid arthritis. As a salve, hyssop treats bruises, insect bites, and bee stings. Hyssop essential oil can help prevent infection.

Magical Uses: This cleansing herb can be used to remove curses, purge negativity, or purify a space. In the home, hyssop protects against thieves and trespassers. Combined with other cleansing herbs like sage, it is useful for smudging to clear away unwanted energies. Planted in the garden it creates a positive energy flow. Hyssop attracts faeries and benevolent natural spirits and keeps wicked spirits at bay.

Personal/Spiritual Growth:
This herb promotes spiritual opening. Add it to bathwater to cleanse the spirit, or burn it to break bad patterns, disengage from negative attachments, and move forward in a positive way. Hyssop essential oil can be used in aromatherapy to calm an anxious mind and bring clarity and focus.

Lemongrass

ORIGINS

Lemongrass (*Cymbopogon citratus*) is an aromatic tropical Asian grass named for its citrusy smell and flavor. The stalks are used in cooking, and the fresh or dried leaves, and the essential oil derived from them, are used in medicine. Lemongrass oil is also used as a pesticide and a preservative.

HISTORY/LORE

Also known as "fever grass," lemongrass has been used to treat fever in India for hundreds of years. Ancient palm-leaf manuscripts found in India were preserved with lemongrass oil. Indigenous Australians used lemongrass as a drink and applied a lemongrass wash to sore eyes, cuts, and skin irritations. Lemongrass appears in many Asian traditional cuisines, including Thai and Vietnamese.

USES

Healing Uses: Lemongrass has antibacterial and antifungal properties, as well as lots of antioxidants. To treat acne, place lemongrass in boiling water, remove from heat, and let the steam wash over the skin. It also has powerful pain-relieving properties, making it useful for headaches, stomachaches, joint pain, and muscle soreness (use the essential oil for these). Lemongrass tea alleviates coughs and soothes sore throats.

Magical Uses: Lemongrass is a powerful cleanser. It removes negativity and brings good luck, making it helpful in spells related to career, love, and family issues. It also increases psychic powers and can be used for psychic cleansing and divination. Use it as a floor wash to clear away evil influences. In the bath, lemongrass leaves have a purifying power.

Personal/Spiritual Growth: Through its cleansing properties, lemongrass removes obstacles and assists in spiritual opening. It enriches communication and helps to make sense of confusing or frustrating situations, particularly with loved ones. As an essential oil, it brings a sense of calm and clarity and also fosters forgiveness—in ourselves and others. Added to bathwater, lemongrass boosts sexual energy. Used in aromatherapy, lemongrass reduces tension and stress and heightens the senses.

Marjoram

ORIGINS

Marjoram (*Origanum majorana*) is a perennial plant in the mint family with small purplish to white flowers and aromatic leaves. Also called sweet marjoram, this plant is native to the Mediterranean region. Its fresh and dried leaves are used for culinary and medicinal purposes. Oregano, a related herb, is sometimes called wild marjoram.

HISTORY/LORE

Marjoram was reportedly one of several herbs found in a 60,000-year-old Neanderthal grave, indicating that the use of this herb is as old as humanity itself. According to Roman mythology, the goddess of love, Venus, gave this plant its scent to remind mortals of her beauty. In Greek mythology, Venus's counterpart, Aphrodite, created marjoram and grew it on Mount Olympus. Aristotle claimed that tortoises ate marjoram after being bitten by snakes, and therefore recommended it as a cure for snakebite.

USES

Healing Uses: As a tea, marjoram eases coughs, colds, and headaches. It also has sedative properties, which can help with insomnia and general tension and stress. Use marjoram essential oil with massage to soothe strains, sprains, and muscle aches. Apply a warm marjoram poultice to ease muscle cramps. Marjoram also boosts the immune system, aids digestion, and calms the stomach.

Magical Uses: Marjoram cleanses, purifies, and removes negativity. Grown in the garden, it protects against evil. Use marjoram in love spells to attract a new lover, enhance a current romantic relationship, or release the grip of a love gone bad. Include marjoram in sachets to attract wealth. Place it under your pillow to bring revealing, meaningful dreams.

Personal/Spiritual Growth: Marjoram has a warming, calming quality, bringing peace to the mind, body, and spirit. It assists those who are grief-stricken by fostering acceptance and clearing the way for happiness. Adding the herb to bathwater is a great way to process grief. Burning marjoram helps you move beyond the past, accept the changes in life, and look to the future.

Parsley

ORIGINS

Parsley (*Petroselinum crispum*) is a biennial Eurasian herb with edible leaves. Varieties include flat-leaf (Italian) parsley and curly-leaf parsley. The leaves have many culinary applications, while both the leaves and the roots are used in medicine. The word *parsley* comes from the Greek *petroselinon*: *petro*, meaning "rock," and *selinon*, meaning celery.

HISTORY/LORE

The ancient Greeks associated parsley with death and used it in funeral ceremonies. One legend says that parsley is slow to germinate because the seed travels to the devil and back nine times before coming up, and any seeds that don't germinate were kept by the devil. Some people are superstitious about transplanting parsley, saying that it brings bad luck.

USES

Healing Uses: Parsley is rich in vitamins C, A, and B as well as iron and calcium. It improves digestion and promotes cardiovascular health. A compress soaked in cooled parsley tea soothes puffiness and swelling. Apply a parsley poultice to insect bites. Parsley essential oil has antibacterial and antifungal properties and can be used to treat acne and skin infections. Parsley root treats urinary and kidney conditions. Chewing on parsley cleans the teeth and freshens the breath. Parsley may be used to bring on menstruation. Pregnant women should not eat large quantities of parsley.

Magical Uses: Use parsley in spells to increase strength and vitality following surgery or an illness. Use a mesh bag of parsley in a purification bath by holding it under the running water. Place parsley on the plate to prevent food contamination. Burn the dried herb as incense in rituals for the dead. Parsley enhances fertility and is often used as an offering to mother goddesses.

Personal/Spiritual Growth: Parsley is an uplifting herb. It restores a sense of well-being and helps the user get out of a rut. Parsley also encourages love and lust, bringing excitement and romance to a relationship.

Peppermint

ORIGINS

Peppermint (*Mentha piperita*) is a cross between watermint and spearmint. This perennial plant has small purple or white flowers and aromatic leaves that are used for both culinary and medicinal purposes. Peppermint is native to Europe and the Middle East, but it is cultivated worldwide.

HISTORY/LORE

Greek mythology offers a creation story for peppermint: Hades, the god of the underworld, seduced a water nymph named Minthe and they entered into a relationship. When Hades's wife, Persephone, found out about the affair, she turned Minthe into a plant so that everyone would walk on her. Hades then gave the plant a pleasant scent, so that every time someone stepped on it they would be reminded of Minthe's beauty.

USES

Healing Uses: Peppermint treats cold and flu, particularly as an expectorant. It is also excellent for digestive issues such as bloating, cramping, diarrhea, nausea, and vomiting (this includes pregnancy-related discomfort). Peppermint contains menthol, a natural analgesic. This, along with selenium and zinc, makes it useful for treating the redness and irritation associated with dandruff. Inhaling the scent of peppermint oil relieves headaches.

Magical Uses: Peppermint is a protective herb. Rub the leaves on furniture or objects or burn dried leaves as incense in a new home to remove any negative energy. Peppermint tea brings passion. Use peppermint in money and prosperity spells. Peppermint essential oil brings alertness in the dream state and assists in remembering and learning from dreams. For this purpose, use it as an inhalation or include the leaves in a sachet placed underneath the pillow.

Personal/Spiritual Growth: Peppermint is a natural stimulant. It boosts energy and invigorates the mind, as well as increases awareness, perception, and sensitivity. Peppermint essential oil cleanses the spirit, increases spiritual attunement, and supports intuition. The essential oil is particularly useful for overcoming resistance to change, as it eliminates fear of the unknown.

Raspberry

ORIGINS

Raspberry (*Rubus idaeus*) is a member of the rose family. Like a rose bush, this plant also has thorny stems. The edible fruit of the raspberry plant may be red, black, purple, or golden, depending on the variety. The leaves also have culinary and medicinal uses.

HISTORY/LORE

As hunter-gatherers, Paleolithic cave dwellers are known to have eaten raspberries. According to Greek mythology, Zeus's nursemaid, Ida, pricked her finger on a thorn of a raspberry bush and her blood dripped onto the fruit, changing it from white to red. Another version of the story says that the berries got their name when the gods found them growing on Mount Ida. (*Rubus idaeus* means "bramble bush of Ida.")

USES

Healing Uses: Raspberry fruit and leaves are used in pregnancy to strengthen uterine tissue, assist with labor, and prevent hemorrhaging during and following birth. Due to its astringent properties, raspberry treats mouth sores, bleeding gums, and other oral inflammation. As a gargle, raspberry soothes sore throats. The fresh or dried leaves can be used in a tea to relieve digestive problems and nausea. Raspberry seed oil benefits the skin and can be used as a natural sunscreen.

Magical Uses: The raspberry plant is associated with fertility. The leaf and fruit can be dried and placed in an amulet to support the female reproductive organs or protect a pregnancy. Steeping the berries in wine and serving it to a lover keeps a relationship strong. Raspberry leaf enhances sleep and brings good dreams.

Personal/Spiritual Growth: First-year raspberry plants do not produce fruit but are essential to the future fertility of the plant. This is a reminder to be patient in creative endeavors, which may take time to fully reach their potential. The thorns of the plant remind us to be gentle with one another.

Rosemary

ORIGINS

Native to the Mediterranean region, rosemary (*Rosmarinus officinalis*) is an aromatic evergreen shrub in the mint family with light bluish-purple flowers and grayish-green, needle-like leaves. The leaves and oil are used for both culinary and medicinal purposes.

HISTORY/LORE

Rosemary has long been associated with immortality, memory, and fidelity. The ancient Egyptians used rosemary in their embalming practices. The ancient Greeks and Romans placed rosemary sprigs in the hands of the dead and burned the herb as incense at funerals. Greek students wore rosemary sprigs in their hair to boost their memories. Rosemary was also incorporated into marriage and baptism ceremonies.

USES

Healing Uses: Rosemary stimulates and strengthens the circulatory and nervous systems, and is used to treat anemia and low blood pressure. Used in a warm poultice, rosemary soothes sore muscles and joint pain. As a salve, rosemary soothes headaches, muscle aches, and swollen feet. Rosemary tea aids digestion. This herb can also be used as a natural insect repellent.

Magical Uses: Rosemary attracts faeries and positive energy and can be used in fidelity spells. Add rosemary to bathwater to improve memory. Burn rosemary during meditation or dream work to remember past lives. Placing rosemary under the pillow assists with dream recall and banishes nightmares and unwanted dream visitations. Rosemary can also be used in purification and cleansing rituals.

Personal/Spiritual Growth: Rosemary is a stimulating, purifying herb. Its memory-boosting properties make it a favorite among students and those whose work requires memorization. Burn rosemary as incense for peace of mind or to cleanse the spirit. For information on the use of rosemary essential oil in aromatherapy, see the rosemary entry in Chapter 4.

Sage

ORIGINS

Sage (*Salvia officinalis*) is a perennial herb in the mint family with blue to purplish flowers and aromatic grayish-green leaves. Native to the Mediterranean region, sage has a long history of culinary and medicinal use. The word *sage* comes from the Latin *salvus*, meaning "healthy." A related herb, clary sage, is covered in Chapter 4: The Power of Scent: Essential Oils.

HISTORY/LORE

According to Greek legend, Cadmus, the founder and first king of Thebes, discovered the medicinal properties of sage when the leaves were offered to him in a religious ceremony. In the Middle Ages, sage was used to treat fevers, liver disease, and epilepsy. It was once believed that young women could use sage in magic to see their future husbands.

USES

Healing Uses: Sage treats many common mouth and throat ailments, including inflamed gums, laryngitis, and tonsillitis. Chewing the leaves cleans the teeth and freshens breath. For sore throats, gargle with sage tea. As a hair wash, sage helps eliminate head lice. Sage's antiseptic qualities make it useful as a compress or salve for treating wounds. As a facial steam bath, sage acts as an astringent for the skin and relieves congestion associated with head colds.

Magical Uses: Sage is used in smudging practices to cleanse a person, object, or space of negative energies or influences. This process, also called "saging," involves burning a bundle of dried sage leaves and letting the smoke waft over the person, object, or space. The smoke attaches to the negative energy and carries it away (be sure to keep windows open when saging to allow smoke to escape).

Personal/Spiritual Growth: Sage is a powerful herb, cleansing both the body and mind of impurities. Burn sage as incense to re-establish physical, spiritual, or emotional balance or to de-stress and relieve anxiety. In aromatherapy, sage essential oil stimulates the mind and relieves mental fatigue and depression.

Saint John's Wort

ORIGINS

Native to Europe and western Asia, Saint John's wort (*Hypericum perforatum*) is a shrubby perennial with bright yellow flowers. When rubbed, the flowers and leaves yield a red oil that has many medicinal uses. This herb gets its name from its connection to Saint John's Day, celebrated in late June. The word *wort* comes from the Old English *wyrt*, meaning "plant."

HISTORY/LORE

Originally a pagan celebration centered on the summer solstice, Saint John's Day, also known as Midsummer, is also a major religious holiday. Depending on the cultural tradition, it may be celebrated any day between June 21 and 25. Christians designated June 24 as the feast day of Saint John the Baptist, but observance begins the day before, known as Saint John's Eve. In medieval Europe, wreaths of Saint John's wort were worn on this holiday and then thrown into bonfires to ensure a plentiful harvest. The herb was also thought to protect against witchcraft.

USES

Healing Uses: The most common medicinal use of Saint John's wort is as a treatment for depression, but it is also used for anxiety, insomnia, and headaches, particularly migraines. An ointment made from the leaves and flowers relieves swelling, muscle cramps, and rheumatism. As a tea, Saint John's wort eases the symptoms of menopause.

Magical Uses: This protective herb can be burned to banish negative influences or used in smudging rituals for exorcism. It is very useful for love spells and divination. Place it under the pillow for romantic, prophetic dreams.

Personal/Spiritual Growth: Saint John's wort brings light in times of darkness and acts as a calming influence. As a flower essence, it stimulates the solar plexus chakra, helping those who feel vulnerable and fearful to find their inner power. Carry Saint John's wort to strengthen your convictions, especially when dealing with confrontations.

Valerian

ORIGINS

Valerian (*Valeriana officinalis*) is a perennial flowering plant native to Eurasia. Its fragrant pink or white flowers are used for flower extracts, and its roots (considered to be rather foul-smelling) are used for various medicinal purposes. The word *valerian* comes from the Latin *Valerianus*, meaning "of Valeria," the Roman province where the plant originated.

HISTORY/LORE

The Greek physician Dioscorides recommended the use of valerian to treat urinary tract infections and as an antidote to poisons. Legend has it that the fabled Pied Piper used valerian to lure rats away from the town of Hamelin, Germany, during the Middle Ages. Valerian was used to treat shell shock in soldiers during World War I.

USES

Healing Uses: Valerian has a tranquilizing and sedative effect on the nervous system, making it excellent for treating insomnia, anxiety, and headaches. It is especially soothing as a tea or added to bathwater. Valerian relaxes the muscles of the gastrointestinal tract and has been used to treat cramping, diarrhea or constipation, flatulence, and irritable bowel syndrome. Note that excessive or prolonged use of valerian may be habit-forming.

Magical Uses: Animals love valerian! Use the root in rituals to evoke animal spirits. Sprinkle powdered valerian root at the front door to deter unwanted visitors. Burn valerian to cleanse and purify a space. Used in bathwater, valerian provides protection from negative influences. Include valerian in a dream pillow to ward off nightmares. As an amulet, valerian provides protection from evil forces and malevolent magic, such as hexes and curses.

Personal/Spiritual Growth: In this area, valerian flower essence is more effective than the root. Unresolved anger and negative emotions can lead to issues including headaches, anxiety, and high blood pressure. Use valerian flower essence in aromatherapy practices to unearth buried feelings of guilt, anger, and negativity and replace them with self-love and acceptance. Valerian also helps you see the positive side of seemingly negative situations.

Yarrow

ORIGINS

Native to Eurasia, yarrow (*Achillea millefolium*), also known as milfoil, is an aromatic perennial with small, feathery leaves and clusters of small, white flowers. The whole plant is used in herbal medicine. The genus *Achillea* gets its name from the Greek hero Achilles, and the species name (*millefolium*) means "thousand leaf."

HISTORY/LORE

According to Greek mythology, the great warrior Achilles used yarrow to treat the wounds of his fellow soldiers during the Trojan War. Yarrow is used in the ancient Chinese system of I Ching divination. It is said that yarrow grows on the grave of the Chinese philosopher Confucius (551–479 B.C.E.) in the Kong Lin Cemetery in China's Shandong province. During the American Civil War, yarrow was used as a surgical dressing to stanch blood flow.

USES

Healing Uses: Yarrow stanches both internal and external bleeding. It is also a common remedy for colds and flu, and it helps to break fevers by promoting perspiration. As a poultice, yarrow treats infections and swelling. Inhaling the steam from yarrow tea calms allergies and aids respiratory problems such as asthma. Applied topically, yarrow essential oil treats wounds; in aromatherapy it relieves stress and tension.

Magical Uses: Yarrow assists with all forms of divination. Drink yarrow tea before divination to help focus the mind and avoid distractions. Yarrow is also useful in love spells and for psychic communication with loved ones. It is especially helpful to newly married couples. Hanging yarrow flowers above the bridal bed ensures that the marriage will last at least seven years. Strewn across the threshold, yarrow protects the home from evil.

Personal/Spiritual Growth: The protective and healing power of yarrow extends to the personal and spiritual realms. It brings courage, clarity, and strength and aids in decision-making. Drink the tea or carry a piece of yarrow with you to enjoy these benefits.

3

THE POWER OF FLOWERS:
Flower Essences

Flower essences are infusions made from the flowering parts of plants aimed at treating the emotional and mental aspects of wellness. Although flower essences have been used in countless cultures all over the world, perhaps the most famous name in the discussion of modern flower essences is Dr. Edward Bach (1886–1936).

Bach was a British physician, homeopath, bacteriologist, and writer best known for developing a form of alternative medicine called Bach flower remedies. Rather than basing these remedies on medical research, he based them on humans' psychic connection to plants. While he recognized the various physical causes of disease, he felt there was also an unseen emotional component to human health. He began to experiment with plants and how they made him feel, and then developed theories about the powers of each one. Bach believed that when early morning sunlight shone on a plant, the light transferred the plant's power to the dewdrops that had collected on its flower petals during the night. He began collecting the dew but soon discovered it did not create a large enough yield. This led him to soak flowers in spring water and place the infusions in sunlight. Thus, Bach flower remedies were born. This chapter contains quotations from Bach's *The Twelve Healers and Other Remedies*.

There are many companies out there that sell Bach's thirty-eight original flower remedies, along with other flower essences and related products. You can also make your own! Flower essences usually come in small dropper bottles and are meant to be taken orally, either on their own or mixed into a beverage. Follow the instructions on the bottle for best results.

Borage

ORIGINS

Native to the Mediterranean region, borage (*Borago officinalis*), also known as starflower, is an annual herb with blue or purplish star-shaped flowers and bristly stems and leaves. The whole plant is edible, but the flowers in particular are favored for their cucumber-like taste, which makes borage flower essence cool and refreshing. It is believed the word *borage* comes from the Arabic *abu araq*, meaning "source of sweat"—due to its use as a sudorific (a substance that cools the body by stimulating the sweat glands).

HISTORY/LORE

The Roman naturalist and philosopher Pliny the Elder (23–79) wrote that borage "maketh a man merry and joyful." Borage is also believed to be the herb called nepenthe in Homer's *Odyssey*—a drug that is supposed to help one forget one's sorrow. Borage flowers steeped in wine was a medieval cure for melancholy.

USES

Borage flower essence is known first and foremost as a courage enhancer, helping you find the inner strength you need to overcome obstacles in life. It brings light and clarity during dark times. Borage soothes the heavyhearted by opening the heart chakra, releasing the emotions that cause depression and making way for optimism, enthusiasm, and joy. Physically, it has a cooling effect, making it a popular addition to summer beverages such as iced tea, lemonade, and fruit juice.

Cherry Plum

ORIGINS

Cherry plum (*Prunus cerasifera*) is a deciduous shrub in the rose family with white flowers and small red or yellow fruit. Both the flowers and the fruit have culinary and medicinal uses, and it is also a popular ornamental shrub. Cherry plum is one of Bach's original flower remedies.

HISTORY/LORE

Not much is known about the history of cherry plum. It is believed to have originated in Asia, and it is now cultivated in Europe and North America as well. Cherry plums are a key ingredient in Georgian cuisine such as tkemali sauce, kharcho soup, and chakapuli stew.

USES

Bach categorized cherry plum under remedies for fear, "fear of the mind being over-strained, of reason giving way, of doing fearful and dreaded things, not wished and known wrong, yet there comes the thought and impulse to do them." This kind of fear can consume one's life, causing depression, damaging personal relationships, and jeopardizing one's career. This flower essence provides assistance to those who live in fear of losing control, losing their minds, or generally "losing it" by providing access to their deep personal reservoirs of inner strength and wisdom. Once in touch with these inner resources, the fearful person can find a way out of the cycle and loosen the grip that fear has on his or her life.

Clematis

ORIGINS

Mainly of Japanese or Chinese origin, *Clematis* is a genus of about 300 species of climbing plants in the buttercup family with flowers or fruit clusters. The name comes from the Greek *klematis*, meaning "twig." Clematis is one of Bach's original flower remedies.

HISTORY/LORE

The Native Americans used clematis as a remedy for migraines, nervous disorders, and skin infections. Early American settlers used clematis as a pepper substitute to spice up food since real pepper was expensive and difficult to obtain.

USES

Bach categorized clematis under "not sufficient interest in present circumstances." He wrote that this flower essence is useful for "those who are dreamy, drowsy, not fully awake, no great interest in life. Quiet people, not really happy in their present circumstances, living more in the future than in the present; living in hopes of happier times, when their ideals may come true. In illness some make little or no effort to get well, and in certain cases may even look forward to death, in the hope of better times; or maybe, meeting again some beloved one whom they have lost." This flower essence brings you back down to earth and into the present so you can live a better life.

Crab Apple

ORIGINS

Malus is a genus of thirty to fifty species of deciduous trees or shrubs that includes the domesticated orchard apple. Native to North America and Eurasia, these trees have clusters of white, pink, or reddish flowers and produce small, tart fruit sometimes used in culinary preparations such as jelly or preserves. Crab apple is one of Bach's original flower remedies.

HISTORY/LORE

The origin of the term *crab apple* is unknown. Theories include the taste of the fruit, which is considered sour and disagreeable (like a crabby person), and the crooked shape of the tree's branches resembling a crab's legs. Some also suggest that it comes from a Norse word meaning "fruit of the wild apple tree."

USES

This flower essence is recommended to those who dislike their appearance or personality or otherwise have a negative self-image. It calms the obsession with those things we don't like about ourselves. Bach categorized it under "for despondency or despair." He wrote: "This is the remedy of cleansing. For those who feel as if they have something not quite clean about themselves. Often it is something of apparently little importance; in others there may be more serious disease which is almost disregarded compared to the one thing on which they concentrate. In both types they are anxious to be free from the one particular thing which is greatest in their minds and which seems so essential to them that it should be cured. They become despondent if treatment fails. Being a cleanser, this remedy purifies wounds if the patient has reason to believe that some poison has entered which must be drawn out."

Dandelion

ORIGINS

As discussed in Chapter 2, dandelion is a perennial plant with bright yellow flowers that is commonly thought of as a weed but also has many medicinal and culinary uses.

HISTORY/LORE

See the dandelion entry in Chapter 2.

USES

Dandelion flower essence connects with the solar plexus chakra, where we store a lot of our issues related to fear, anger, and self-worth. It helps you release negative feelings toward yourself and others, and battles addictive and compulsive behaviors and thoughts. This flower essence assists those who feel like they are caught in a cycle and therefore can't enjoy the natural flow of life. It teaches these individuals to listen closely to their own personal needs and live in a more effortless, natural way.

Forget-Me-Not

ORIGINS

Forget-me-nots include a number of species of flowering plants of the genus *Myosotis*. The plant's name is borrowed from the German *Vergissmeinnicht*, and its small blue flowers have many uses in herbal medicine.

HISTORY/LORE

According to legend, during medieval times, a knight was walking next to a river with his beloved and bent down to pick flowers for her. He lost his balance and fell into the river, and his heavy armor started to drag him under. Before drowning, he tossed the flowers up to his lady and shouted, "Forget me not!" As a result, it is believed that those who wear this flower will never be forgotten by their lovers.

USES

When we feel that our world is small, it makes us feel lost and alone. Forget-me-not flower essence calms and comforts by bringing you into contact with the larger spiritual world and connecting you to other levels of consciousness. As a result, it enhances personal relationships. In some cases, it may restore a connection to a lost loved one. This flower essence offers guidance and a sense of purpose, as well as a feeling that everything is connected.

Gentian

ORIGINS

Gentiana is a large genus of flowering plants with about 400 species. Native to temperate regions of Asia, Europe, and the Americas, these plants are known for their blue, trumpet-shaped flowers. Gentian is one of Bach's original flower remedies.

HISTORY/LORE

Gentian most likely gets its name from Gentius, an Illyrian king who ruled during the second century B.C.E. and who may have been the first to discover the plant's medicinal properties. According to legend, in the eleventh century, the Hungarian king Ladislaus prayed for divine help with a disease that was afflicting his subjects. He then shot an arrow into the air, and when he found it, it was embedded in a gentian root, which proved to be the remedy needed to cure the disease.

USES

Bach categorized gentian under "for those who suffer uncertainty" and recommended the flower essence for "those who are easily discouraged. They may be progressing well in illness or in the affairs of their daily life, but any small delay or hindrance to progress causes doubt and soon disheartens them." It lifts that downhearted feeling we get when things go wrong and speeds up the process of bouncing back from setbacks.

Gorse

ORIGINS

Gorse is any of the flowering plants of the genus *Ulex*, which comprises about twenty species of thorny evergreen shrubs. Native to Europe, these plants have fragrant, edible yellow flowers and black pods. Gorse is one of Bach's original flower remedies.

HISTORY/LORE

Gorse was brought to New Zealand in the 1830s, and it rapidly took over areas of cleared land and farmland. Over time it became known as an invasive weed, and great sums of money have been spent on controlling its spread. It is estimated that gorse covers between 3 and 5 percent of New Zealand's total land area.

USES

Bach categorized gorse under "for those who suffer uncertainty" and recommended the flower essence for those suffering from "very great hopelessness, they have given up belief that more can be done for them. Under persuasion or to please others they may try different treatments, at the same time assuring those around that there is so little hope of relief." This flower essence shines a light on the path out of despair, restoring one's faith and helping one to move forward.

Honeysuckle

ORIGINS

Honeysuckle is a shrub or vine belonging to the genus *Lonicera* with fragrant, tubular flowers and small berries. The genus gets its name from the German botanist Adam Lonicer (1528–1586). Honeysuckle is one of Bach's original flower remedies.

HISTORY/LORE

There are many varieties of honeysuckle, including Japanese honeysuckle, orange honeysuckle, and coral honeysuckle. Japanese honeysuckle was introduced to the United States in the early to mid-1800s for ornamental use and as a soil stabilizer. Orange honeysuckle attracts hummingbirds. The Native Americans smoked the dried leaves of coral honeysuckle to relieve the symptoms of asthma.

USES

Bach categorized honeysuckle under "not sufficient interest in present circum-stances." He recommended this flower essence for "those who live much in the past, perhaps a time of great happiness, or memories of a lost friend, or ambi-tions which have not come true. They do not expect further happiness such as they have had." This flower essence helps us learn from rather than live in the past, showing us that there is much to look forward to. This is also good for homesickness and nostalgia.

Impatiens

ORIGINS

Impatiens is a very large genus of between 800 and 1,000 species of flowering plants of the balsam family widely cultivated for their colorful flowers. Handle this plant and you'll see where it gets its name—the ripe seedpods burst open when touched. Impatiens is one of Bach's original flower remedies.

HISTORY/LORE

Impatiens were discovered growing in eastern Africa and are believed to have originated in Zanzibar, an island off the coast of present-day Tanzania. The British physician and naturalist John Kirk introduced impatiens to the Western world in 1896.

USES

Bach categorized impatiens under "loneliness" and wrote that this flower essence is helpful to "those who are quick in thought and action and who wish all things to be done without hesitation or delay. When ill they are anxious for a hasty recovery. They find it very difficult to be patient with people who are slow as they consider it wrong and a waste of time, and they will endeavour to make such people quicker in all ways. They often prefer to work and think alone, so that they can do everything at their own speed." This flower essence helps us relax, slow down, and understand that things take time. It also encourages us to be more accepting when dealing with others.

Lily

ORIGINS

Lily is a plant of the genus *Lilium* that grows from a bulb and has large, often trumpet-shaped flowers. The flowers can be a variety of colors and are usually fragrant. Alpine lily, calla lily, Easter lily, and mariposa lily are just a few of the many varieties of this plant.

HISTORY/LORE

According to biblical lore, lilies were found growing in Gethsemane after Christ died—the garden where Jesus prayed and the apostles slept the night before the crucifixion. In China, several lily species are cultivated as root vegetables. Lily root is also featured in Japanese cuisine, especially as an ingredient in chawan-mushi, a savory egg custard.

USES

Alpine lily flower essence helps women integrate all sides of their feminine identities and stay grounded in their bodies. Calla lily flower essence expands one's notion of sexual identity and is best taken with a partner. Easter lily flower essence manages the tension between sexuality and spirituality. Mariposa lily flower essence enables us to act as mothers to ourselves, healing feelings of separation and alienation and bringing comfort, joy, and freedom.

Red Clover

ORIGINS

Red clover (*Trifolium pratense*) is a Eurasian perennial with rose-colored flowers and trifoliate leaves (hence the genus name). It is largely used as a cover crop, to protect and enrich the soil, and is also a favorite of grazing farm animals. The idiom "in clover" describes a carefree life of ease, comfort, and prosperity.

HISTORY/LORE

In ancient China, dried red clover was burned at altars as incense. Medieval Christians associated this plant's three-part leaves with the holy trinity. There is a long history of red clover being used to treat cancer, specifically breast, ovarian, and lymphatic cancers. Red clover became the state flower of Vermont in 1895.

USES

When mass consciousness threatens your sense of identity, red clover flower essence keeps you firmly rooted in your beliefs. It supports self-awareness and helps you locate and act from your own center of truth. This flower essence also encourages a calm demeanor in crisis situations. Turn to it in times when cleansing or balancing is needed.

Rose

ORIGINS

The genus *Rosa* comprises many species of shrubs and vines with prickly stems and fragrant flowers. Most species are native to Asia, although some are native to Europe, North America, and northwestern Africa. The Latin *rosa* may be an Etruscan form of the Greek *Rhodia*, meaning "originating from Rhodes"—a Greek city. Rock rose and wild rose are two of Bach's original flower remedies.

HISTORY/LORE

Ornamental roses were cultivated in the Mediterranean, Persia, and China as early as 500 B.C.E. The French empress Joséphine de Beauharnais (1763–1814) adored roses and maintained a famous rose garden at her Château de Malmaison. Prior to her marriage to Napoleon, she was known by the name Rose.

USES

Bach categorized rock rose under "for those who have fear" and recommended the flower essence as "the remedy of emergency for cases where there even appears no hope. In accident or sudden illness, or when the patient is very frightened or terrified, or if the condition is serious enough to cause great fear to those around. If the patient is not conscious the lips may be moistened with the remedy." He categorized wild rose under "not sufficient interest in present circumstances" and recommended the flower essence to "those who without apparently sufficient reason become resigned to all that happens, and just glide through life, take it as it is, without any effort to improve things and find some joy. They have surrendered to the struggle of life without complaint."

Star of Bethlehem

ORIGINS

Star of Bethlehem may be any of the plants of the genus *Ornithogalum*, which grow from a bulb and have star-shaped white flowers. Some of the plants of this genus are edible and eaten as vegetables, while others are poisonous. Native to the Mediterranean region, star of Bethlehem is one of Bach's original flower remedies.

HISTORY/LORE

This plant is named for the star that guided the magi to Bethlehem to see the baby Jesus. Because of its biblical name, it has come to be associated with purity, hope, love, and happiness. It is also a popular choice for religious ceremonies, weddings, and romantic gestures.

USES

This is the flower essence for those unexpected, unfortunate events in life. Bach categorized star of Bethlehem under "for despondency or despair" and suggested it "for those in great distress under conditions which for a time produce great unhappiness. The shock of serious news, the loss of someone dear, the fright following an accident, and such like. For those who for a time refuse to be consoled, this remedy brings comfort." Trauma can have long-lasting negative effects on the mind, body, and spirit. Star of Bethlehem flower essence uncovers unresolved issues resulting from trauma so that they can be dealt with before they begin to manifest in other harmful ways.

Sunflower

ORIGINS

The genus *Helianthus* comprises about seventy species of sunflowers, most of which are native to North America; a few are native to South America. This tall plant has a large, round, yellow flower head with petals reminiscent of the rays of the sun. The name comes from the Greek: *helios* (sun) plus *anthos* (flower).

HISTORY/LORE

Evidence suggests that Native Americans cultivated sunflowers in present-day Arizona and New Mexico as early as 3000 B.C.E., perhaps even before corn. They ate the seeds, ground them to make flour, and extracted oil from them. The Incas of South America treasured the flower for its resemblance to the sun and associated it with Inti, the sun god. The Spanish brought sunflowers to Europe in the 1500s.

USES

Sunflower flower essence harnesses our inner radiance and lets it shine outward. It helps to balance the crown chakra, which controls mental energy and is our connection to the divine. It also fosters courage and self-confidence in those of us who mask our true selves hoping for love and acceptance. This flower essence celebrates each of us as a unique individual.

151

4

THE POWER OF SCENT:
Essential Oils

Essential oils are liquids that are extracted from aromatic plants and then used for healing and therapeutic practices, known collectively as aromatherapy. These fragrant oils are what draw bees to flowers and cause you to stop and smell the roses. The ancient Egyptians, Greeks, and Romans were the first to use aromatic plant oils in baths and massage for healing and therapeutic purposes, and these practices are still widely used in modern aromatherapy.

The French chemist and scholar René-Maurice Gattefossé (1881–1950) is considered the father of aromatherapy. His fascination with essential oils began in the early 1900s when he was working at his family's cosmetics company, which is still in business. He later used essential oils to treat the wounds of soldiers during World War I. The Austrian-born biochemist Marguerite Maury (1895–1968) subsequently developed massage techniques incorporating essential oils that are still in use today.

Essential oils are powerful, highly concentrated substances, and most have to be diluted in a carrier oil (such as sweet almond, jojoba, or grape seed) before use. Some essential oils can be applied directly to the skin, while others should only be used for their aromas. Always follow the instructions on the bottle, making sure not to exceed the recommended number of drops in each application, and don't ever swallow essential oils. To maximize their shelf life, keep oils in a cool, dark place, either at cool room temperature or in the refrigerator. If you keep them in the fridge, place them in a sealed container to prevent the fragrance from affecting food. On average, essential oils will keep for six months to a year if kept cool. If oil becomes cloudy or begins to smell sour, throw it away.

Balsam

ORIGINS

Balsam is an aromatic tree resin that is used to make a variety of popular essential oils. These include balsam fir, whose aroma brings to mind a Christmas tree, and balsam of Peru, which smells like vanilla and cinnamon due to the presence of vanillin and cinnamic acid. Balsam of Peru comes from a tree of the genus *Myroxylon* grown in Central and South America, primarily in El Salvador.

HISTORY/LORE

Balsam of Peru is a misnomer. Although balsam was collected all over Central and South America, it was shipped to Europe from Peru—hence the name. The first recorded export of balsam of Peru to Europe occurred in the seventeenth century. Long before that, the Maya were using balsam of Peru as incense for medicinal purposes.

USES

Healing Uses: Balsam fir essential oil soothes muscle aches and pains resulting from exercise, and also aids the respiratory system. Balsam of Peru essential oil treats skin conditions, rheumatism, and respiratory issues, particularly those accompanied by a productive cough. It also has antiseptic and anti-inflammatory properties, making it helpful for healing wounds. However, balsam of Peru is one of the most prevalent allergies, so proceed with caution when trying it for the first time.

Personal/Spiritual Growth: Balsam fir essential oil stimulates the mind while relaxing the body, creating a general sense of well-being. This is a wonderful essential oil for moody people, as it serves to regulate and balance the forces within the body. It is especially helpful for balancing the sacral and heart chakras. During meditation, it serves as a grounding influence. Balsam of Peru essential oil reduces stress and mental exhaustion, but be aware that it may also bring up negative emotions that have been buried.

Basil

ORIGINS

Basil essential oil comes from the familiar culinary and medicinal herb discussed in Chapter 2. Varieties include sweet basil and holy basil, which are similar in appearance but have their own individual properties and uses. Sweet basil has a fresh, herbaceous aroma, while holy basil has a strong, spicy fragrance.

HISTORY/LORE

Holy basil, or *tulsi*, is native to India and is considered sacred in the Hindu religion. Hindus regard the plant as a manifestation of the goddess Tulsi and traditionally keep a holy basil plant in or near their homes. In Crete, basil was placed on windowsills to keep the devil away.

USES

Healing Uses: Rub sweet basil essential oil on the abdomen to relieve indigestion, nausea, or stomach cramps. As an inhalation, both sweet basil and holy basil essential oils can be used to treat coughs, congestion, asthma, bronchitis, and sinus infections. Combined with massage, these oils relieve muscle aches and soreness.

Personal/Spiritual Growth: Inhaling the scent of basil refreshes and energizes the mind and eases headaches brought on by stress and tension. Sweet basil essential oil gives you the courage you need when undertaking new experiences. It also helps to clarify goals and plans. Holy basil essential oil opens your heart to receive the love of your partner, and it fortifies your sense of purpose, enabling you to focus on life's possibilities.

Bergamot

ORIGINS

Bergamot essential oil comes from the rind of the citrus fruit of the bergamot tree (*Citrus bergamia*), which is commercially grown in southern Italy. The fruit is generally not eaten due to its sour flavor, but the oil has a fresh citrusy/floral scent. The word *bergamot* comes from Bergamo, a city in northern Italy where the tree was first cultivated.

HISTORY/LORE

Although it takes its name from an Italian city, the bergamot tree is actually native to Southeast Asia. Bergamot essential oil was first used in perfumes and cosmetics, and it was later valued for its medicinal properties. The oil is also an important ingredient in Earl Grey tea.

USES

Healing Uses: Bergamot essential oil stimulates the mind and body, and aids in circulation and digestion. Applied topically, it heals cuts, acne, cold sores, and psoriasis. Just be sure to avoid the sun for twenty-four hours after applying bergamot essential oil to the skin, as exposure to UV rays can cause discoloration of the skin or sunburn.

Personal/Spiritual Growth: The scent of bergamot essential oil has a balancing, regenerating, and uplifting effect. It builds confidence and enhances your mood, while helping you overcome obstacles and paving the way for new opportunities and growth. It is especially valuable for those dealing with depression, stress, tension, or fear. Use with massage or add to bathwater in these cases.

Carnation

ORIGINS

Carnation essential oil comes from the familiar flower (*Dianthus caryophyllus*), which is native to the Mediterranean region. The oil has a mildly sweet scent with notes of honey and spice, and it is typically found in "absolute" form, meaning that it was extracted using chemical solvents. The word *carnation* comes from the Latin *carnatio*, meaning "flesh."

HISTORY/LORE

Flowers of the genus *Dianthus* are also known as "pinks." The word *pink* comes from the Middle English *pinken*, meaning "to push or prick," a reference to the flower petals' jagged edges. The creation of carnation perfume is attributed to American perfumer Mary Chess, who, after becoming dissatisfied with commercial "toilet waters," began making her own fragrances using all natural ingredients in the early 1930s.

USES

Healing Uses: As a massage oil, carnation heals, softens, and rejuvenates the skin, and its soothing fragrance promotes relaxation. It treats a variety of skin conditions, including eczema and rosacea, and soothes rashes and other irritations. It brings energy and strength to those suffering from illness. This essential oil can also be used as an antidepressant or to treat sleeplessness.

Personal/Spiritual Growth: This essential oil is spiritually uplifting and motivating. It fosters a feeling of openness and oneness with the universe, allowing the soul to relax and luxuriate in all experiences. Carnation essential oil facilitates contact with the deepest parts of ourselves so that we may sort through buried emotions and locate our true desires. It is also a powerful aphrodisiac.

Cedar

ORIGINS

Cedar essential oil comes from the bark of the cedar tree, a coniferous evergreen that is native to the western Himalayas and the Mediterranean. Also called cedarwood, this oil has a woody, balsamic fragrance. Cedar wood is a natural moth repellent, which is why it is often used to make chests or closets for clothing storage.

HISTORY/LORE

The ancient Egyptians used cedar oil in the embalming process and as a perfume, and they used the wood to make sarcophagi. The ancient Greeks and Romans burned cedar as incense. Cedar is mentioned in both the Bible and the Talmud. The Native Americans used cedar to enhance spiritual communication.

USES

Healing Uses: Cedar essential oil is high in sesquiterpenes, natural compounds that stimulate the limbic system of the brain, which controls mood. For this reason, cedar oil is used in aromatherapy to reduce stress, assist with sleep, and support relaxation. This oil has antiseptic and anti-inflammatory properties, making it useful for treating skin issues and wounds. Rubbed on the joints, it soothes arthritis pain.

Personal/Spiritual Growth: This essential oil works with the heart chakra to bring self-acceptance and love. It banishes fear and instills a feeling of safety and security in yourself and in your environment. In addition to promoting relaxation, cedar essential oil may also improve focus and encouragement in the pursuit of long-held dreams and desires.

Cinnamon

ORIGINS

Like the spice included in Chapter 2, cinnamon essential oil comes from certain tropical Asian trees of the genus *Cinnamomum*. There are two main varieties of this oil, one that comes from the leaves and one that comes from the bark, each with its own properties and uses. Both have a warm, spicy aroma, although the leaf oil is milder while the bark oil is more intense.

HISTORY/LORE

Despite cinnamon's widespread use throughout the ancient world, the Arab merchants who transported it managed to keep its origins secret until the early sixteenth century. European explorers, including Christopher Columbus and Gonzalo Pizzaro, set out in search of the spice's source, and Portuguese traders finally discovered cinnamon in Ceylon (present-day Sri Lanka) around 1518.

USES

Healing Uses: This essential oil supports cardiovascular and immune health and has a general calming effect. Cinnamon bark oil contains aldehydes, which soothe the nervous system. Eugenol, found in cinnamon leaf oil, has antiseptic and anesthetic properties. Used around the home, this oil battles mold and bacteria, improving air quality. Plus, it smells great! Note that some people are allergic to cinnamon, and those with sensitive skin may find its "spicy" effect irritating.

Personal/Spiritual Growth: Cinnamon essential oil provides warmth, comfort, and mild stimulation. It opens the solar plexus chakra and allows you to release old anger, resentment, frustration, and fear. This oil is perfect for those who want to let go of the past and break old patterns. It also combats depression and addiction. Cinnamon leaf oil in particular boosts motivation and creativity.

Clary Sage

ORIGINS

Like the herb discussed in Chapter 2, clary sage is a plant in the genus *Salvia* that is native to the Mediterranean region. Clary sage essential oil comes from the leaves of this plant and is commonly used as a flavoring, in perfumery, and of course, in aromatherapy. It has an earthy, herbaceous aroma.

HISTORY/LORE

The ancient Greek botanist and philosopher Theophrastus (371–287 B.C.E.) wrote extensively about the medicinal uses of clary sage. During the Middle Ages, clary sage was called "clear eye," due to the belief that it improved vision and protected the eyes from the effects of aging. In sixteenth-century England, this plant was sometimes substituted for hops in the production of beer.

USES

Healing Uses: This is an excellent essential oil for women, as it assists with menstrual issues, childbirth, and symptoms of menopause, including mood swings. (Note that it should be avoided during the first months of pregnancy.) For cramps, massage the oil into the abdomen or lower back. Clary sage essential oil also benefits the skin and hair. Inhaling the scent has a calming effect and helps battle anxiety and depression.

Personal/Spiritual Growth: If you suffer from a racing mind, this oil is for you. It helps keep you relaxed and focused, so you can be in the present and go with the flow. This allows you to access inner wisdom without the distraction of too much thought. Clary sage essential oil opens the root and sacral chakras, grounding the spirit in the body and boosting self-confidence and self-worth. It is also a powerful aphrodisiac and may enhance dreaming.

Clove

ORIGINS

Like the spice discussed in Chapter 2, clove essential oil comes from the flower bud of the evergreen tree *Syzygium aromaticum*. Clove leaf oil is also used, but its effect is milder than that of the flower bud. This essential oil has a sweet, spicy fragrance.

HISTORY/LORE

Cloves were found in Syrian pottery dating back to 1720 B.C.E. It was once believed that cinnamon was the bark, clove was the flower, and nutmeg was the fruit of the same tree. Cloves were one of the "big four" most valuable spices during the medieval era, along with nutmeg, cinnamon, and pepper.

USES

Healing Uses: Clove boosts the immune and digestive systems and offers antioxidant support. Like cinnamon, clove contains large amounts of eugenol, a natural antiseptic and anesthetic. Eugenol is used in the dental industry to numb the gums. To stimulate circulation and soothe muscular pain, rub clove essential oil on the affected area.

Personal/Spiritual Growth: Clove gets to the root of pain and discomfort—physical or emotional. It works with the solar plexus, heart, and throat chakras to fortify the self, expand inner strength and vision, and draw out personal truth. Once the truth has emerged, you will feel inspired to take action in that direction.

Eucalyptus

ORIGINS

This essential oil comes from the leaves of the eucalyptus tree (*Eucalyptus globulus*), which is native to Australia and cultivated worldwide. The oil has a clean, medicinal scent—think Vicks VapoRub. The word *eucalyptus* comes from the Greek *kaluptos*, meaning "covered"—an allusion to the tree's capped flower bud.

HISTORY/LORE

Scientists estimate that the eucalyptus tree has survived on Earth for 50 million years. Indigenous Australians have been using the branches of this ancient tree to make a ceremonial wind instrument called the didgeridoo for the past 1,500 years. The British botanist Sir Joseph Banks (1743–1820) is credited with introducing eucalyptus to the Western world.

USES

Healing Uses: Eucalyptus leaves are rich in eucalyptol, a natural compound often used in mouthwashes and cough suppressants. Use eucalyptus essential oil with massage to soothe sore muscles, or rub it on the chest to clear up productive coughs and congestion. In some cases, it may ease the symptoms of asthma. This oil is an effective insect repellent, and can be used to treat insect bites and stings.

Personal/Spiritual Growth: This essential oil acts as a mental stimulant, battling exhaustion and sluggishness and boosting positive energy. A whiff of its fresh scent instantly rejuvenates the spirit, bringing relief to those struggling from melancholy or depression. It also encourages emotional balance. To clear a cluttered mind, add it to bathwater. Eucalyptus essential oil opens the solar plexus and heart chakras.

Frankincense

ORIGINS

Frankincense is the aromatic resin of trees of the genus *Boswellia*, native to Africa and Asia. The word comes from the Old French *franc encens*: *franc*, meaning "free" or "pure," and *encens*, meaning "incense." *Incense* comes from the Latin verb *incendere*, "to set on fire." Frankincense essential oil has a woody, balsamic scent.

HISTORY/LORE

The ancient Egyptians used frankincense as incense, perfume, a cosmetic ingredient, an embalming preservative, and an offering to the gods. In the Bible, frankincense is one of the three gifts the wise men bring to the baby Jesus; the other two are gold and myrrh (see entry in this chapter).

USES

Healing Uses: This essential oil benefits the skin and battles signs of premature aging. It soothes sunburns, heals rashes, and prevents scarring, and it can also reduce the appearance of stretch marks. As an inhalation, it treats bronchitis. To ease joint and muscle pain, rub frankincense essential oil on the affected area.

Personal/Spiritual Growth: Frankincense essential oil drives away negativity and brings peace and balance. This is a wonderful oil for meditation, as it helps with grounding, clears your mind, and deepens your spiritual connections. It also enhances visions. Once you connect with your spiritual side, you can recognize and pursue your true purpose. Add this oil to bathwater when you feel overwhelmed.

Gardenia

ORIGINS

Native to China, *Gardenia* is a genus of tropical shrubs and trees with glossy green leaves and fragrant white flowers. The oil, which has a sweet, floral scent, comes from the flowers of *Gardenia jasminoides*, but the roots and leaves also have medicinal uses.

HISTORY/LORE

This flower is named after Alexander Garden (1730–1791), a Scottish physician, botanist, and zoologist. It was previously, and is sometimes still, known as Cape jasmine. Dried gardenia flowers have long been used in Chinese herbal medicine to treat anxiety, draw heat away from the body, and reduce swelling.

USES

Healing Uses: This essential oil can be used as an anti-inflammatory, an antidepressant, or a sedative. It treats tension and headaches, and may reduce symptoms of menopause. It can also ease dizziness. Added to bathwater, it has a relaxing effect and prevents insomnia. As an inhalation, gardenia essential oil eases respiratory issues, including sinus infections. Applied topically, it treats wounds and reduces swelling.

Personal/Spiritual Growth: Gardenia essential oil fosters love and harmony and works to improve mood. Add it to bathwater to ease a troubled mind. Use it with massage to bring peace and serenity. This oil stimulates the heart chakra and can also be used as an aphrodisiac, particularly in women.

Geranium

ORIGINS

This essential oil comes from the leaves of the geranium plant, a member of the genus *Pelargonium*,
which comprises hundreds of species. One of the most
prominent sources of this essential oil is *Pelargonium gra-
veolens*, native to the island of Réunion in the Indian Ocean.
Although the oil comes from the leaves and not the flowers, the
fragrance is often compared to that of a rose.

HISTORY/LORE

There are actually two genera of geraniums: *Pelargonium* and *Geranium*. When
the Swedish botanist Carl Linnaeus (1707–1778) created his plant taxonomy, he
grouped all of these plants together. The genera have since been separated, but
both are still generally known as geraniums. These plants are sometimes called
storksbill or cranesbill, due to the beak-like shape of the seed capsule.

USES

Healing Uses: This essential oil
supports the circulatory and nervous
systems, and it is also excellent for
the skin. It heals wounds and treats a
number of skin conditions, including
acne, eczema, and athlete's foot. Use it
as an insect repellent or to relieve the
itch and discomfort of insect bites. As
a massage oil, it soothes sore muscles.

Personal/Spiritual Growth:
Geranium essential oil has a strong
feminine energy. It soothes and nur-
tures the inner child, fostering a sense
of calm and peace. It lifts the spirit
and helps to release negative memories and stress. This essential oil provides comfort and reassurance in
times of distress or disappointment.
Added to bathwater, this oil eases irritability. An inhalation before bed will
relax the mind and prevent insomnia.

Jasmine

ORIGINS

Jasmine essential oil comes from the fragrant white or yellow flowers of vines or shrubs of the genus *Jasminum*, mainly *Jasminum officinale*, which are native to Asia. In this case, *essential oil* is a misnomer, as the flowers are too delicate to withstand the distillation process. Instead, this oil is an absolute, which means it is extracted using chemical solvents. It is rather expensive due to the large number of flowers needed to produce it. This oil has a strong, sweet, floral aroma.

HISTORY/LORE

Jasmine absolute is called the king of oils (rose is the queen). A related plant, *Jasminum sambac*, is very important in India. It is incorporated into cultural traditions and ceremonies, and women often wear the blossoms in their hair. Jasmine is the national flower of Pakistan, where it is known as *chameli*. Jasmine tea is extremely popular in China.

USES

Healing Uses: This oil eases cramps and mood swings associated with PMS and menstruation. It is too strong to be used during pregnancy, but it is excellent for childbirth (use it to massage the lower abdomen during labor). Jasmine absolute benefits the skin and acts as an antidepressant. It is also a well-known aphrodisiac.

Personal/Spiritual Growth: Jasmine oil is associated with female energy, particularly sexual energy. It promotes the expression of intimate feelings and enhances sexual vitality. It also boosts confidence and has a general uplifting quality. In times of confusion, jasmine essential oil brings the true wishes of the heart to light. Add to bathwater to relieve stress.

Lavender

ORIGINS

A flowering plant in the mint family, lavender (*Lavandula angustifolia*) is the quintessential aromatherapy plant. Its refreshing floral scent makes for a relaxing essential oil, and it also has many medicinal and household uses. Lavender is native to the Mediterranean region.

HISTORY/LORE

The ancient Greeks used lavender in embalming practices. The ancient Greeks and Romans used lavender for healing as well as for cleansing purposes. In 1910, while working in the lab at his family's cosmetics company, the French chemist and scholar René-Maurice Gattefossé (1881–1950) burned his hand and then plunged it into the nearest tub of liquid, lavender essential oil. Later, he was astonished to see how quickly his burn healed, and with very little scarring.

USES

Healing Uses: The scent of lavender is extremely relaxing. It relieves headaches, tension, anxiety, and insomnia, making it a wonderful addition to bathwater or a pillow. Applied topically, this oil heals wounds, burns, eczema, acne, and other skin irritations. With massage, it soothes muscle aches and reduces swelling.

Personal/Spiritual Growth: This is the ultimate essential oil for peace and calm, allowing for relaxation and restful sleep. It lifts the spirit and brings emotional balance with its nurturing, reassuring quality. This makes it especially helpful to those dealing with depression. Lavender unblocks the third eye chakra, quieting the mind and facilitating higher states of awareness.

Lemon

ORIGINS

Lemon essential oil comes from the peel of the yellow fruit of the evergreen tree *Citrus limon*, which is native to Asia and cultivated in the southern Mediterranean region. This oil has a fresh, citrusy fragrance and many therapeutic, medicinal, and household uses.

HISTORY/LORE

The exact origin of the lemon tree is undetermined, but many think it may have been northwestern India. Arab traders then brought the plant to the Middle East and Africa, and from there it traveled to Europe. Until about the tenth century, the lemon tree was mainly an ornamental plant. After that, it developed culinary and medicinal uses, such as a treatment for scurvy, a disease resulting from a deficiency of vitamin C.

USES

Healing Uses: Lemon essential oil has antiseptic and astringent qualities, making it excellent for the skin as well as household cleaning. It boosts energy, fights fatigue, and improves mood. It also calms the stomach, relieves nausea, and improves digestion. Avoid sun exposure after topical use of this oil, as it can "bleach" hair and cause skin irritation such as blisters and burns.

Personal/Spiritual Growth: One whiff of this uplifting essential oil clears away negative emotions and fosters a cheerful mood. It serves to purify the mind, body, and soul. It also enhances focus and concentration and helps with problem solving and decision-making. Lemon oil balances the solar plexus chakra.

Mint

ORIGINS

Mint essential oil comes from the leaves of plants of the genus *Mentha*, including peppermint (*Mentha piperita*), spearmint (*Mentha spicata*), and bergamot mint (*Mentha citrata*). Most will recognize the fresh, sharp aroma of this essential oil as that of chewing gum, toothpaste, liniments for sore muscles, and other common products.

HISTORY/LORE

The word *mint* comes from the Greek *minthe*, which is also the name of a nymph in Greek mythology. According to the story, Mentha angered Persephone, who turned her into a pungent plant as punishment. Native to Europe, Asia, and Australia, mint plants are cultivated in temperate regions worldwide.

USES

Healing Uses: Mint essential oil contains menthol, a natural compound that acts as a topical anesthetic. Rub on sore muscles to cool and soothe the area, or on the abdomen to relieve intestinal discomfort. This oil eases nausea, calms stomach cramps, and supports digestion. It also alleviates stress and conditions resulting from stress, such as headaches and insomnia.

Personal/Spiritual Growth: This essential oil refreshes and revives the spirit, eliminating fatigue and boosting energy. Peppermint oil supports awareness and replaces negativity with positivity. Spearmint oil cools heated emotions and brings inner peace and calm. Bergamot mint oil inspires spontaneity. Add any of these to bathwater for emotional balance.

Myrrh

ORIGINS

Myrrh is the aromatic gum resin of trees and shrubs of the genus *Commiphora*, native to northeastern Africa and the Middle East. Historically, it has been used to make perfume, incense, and medicine. Myrrh essential oil has a rich, woody aroma.

HISTORY/LORE

The ancient Egyptians used myrrh in embalming practices. The first known medical use of myrrh (topical application to wounds) is documented in a Greek text dating back to the fifth century B.C.E. In the Bible, myrrh is one of the three gifts the wise men bring to the baby Jesus; the other two are gold and frankincense (see entry in this chapter).

USES

Healing Uses: Myrrh essential oil supports the circulatory, nervous, and digestive systems. It also eases chest congestion and coughs; for this purpose, use it as an inhalation or rub it on the chest. This oil has astringent, antiseptic, and anti-inflammatory properties, making it helpful for treating wounds. In a hot compress, it draws out infection.

Personal/Spiritual Growth: The high levels of sesquiterpenes in myrrh essential oil stimulate the brain's limbic system, which controls mood. Inhaling the fragrance of this oil has a calming and uplifting effect, fostering a sense of peace and tranquility. It encourages letting go of old wounds and allows for the forgiveness that is necessary for moving forward. Use in meditation to establish spiritual balance.

Orange Blossom

ORIGINS

Orange blossom essential oil, also called neroli, comes from the flower of the bitter orange tree *Citrus aurantium*. Like lemon essential oil, it has therapeutic, medicinal, and household uses. The oil has a sweet, citrusy fragrance.

HISTORY/LORE

The ancient Egyptians used orange blossom oil for healing and ceremonial purposes. French-born Marie Anne de la Trémoille (1642–1722), a princess of Nerola, Italy, is credited with introducing bitter orange oil as a fashionable fragrance; hence the name neroli. It has been said that this oil is one of the ingredients in the secret recipe for the soft drink Coca-Cola.

USES

Healing Uses: Orange blossom essential oil supports the digestive and nervous systems and benefits the skin. Rub it on the abdomen to ease indigestion, and massage it into dry areas to moisturize and rejuvenate skin. As an inhalation, it is an effective treatment for insomnia or disrupted sleep, and it can lift depression and relieve anxiety.

Personal/Spiritual Growth: This rich essential oil fosters happiness and revitalizes the spirit. It opens the sacral chakra, the source of confidence and self-worth. It releases insecurities and fosters a sense of inner peace and harmony. Keeping your mind and body firmly rooted in the present, it allows you to harness your own personal power to manifest your desires. Enjoy it added to bathwater.

Patchouli

ORIGINS

This essential oil comes from the leaves of the shrub *Pogostemon cablin*, a member of the mint family. Native to Southeast Asia, this plant is extensively cultivated in India, Malaysia, China, Indonesia, the Philippines, and South America. The oil has a musky, earthy aroma.

HISTORY/LORE

In the eighteenth and nineteenth centuries, Indian silk traders packed their cloth in patchouli to keep moths away, leading many to believe that the cloth itself had a rich scent. Both patchouli oil and incense became enormously popular in the United States and Europe during the hippie movement of the 1960s and 1970s.

USES

Healing Uses: Patchouli essential oil is an excellent remedy for skin issues. It hydrates and nourishes dry, chapped skin and clears up conditions such as acne and eczema. Applied to the hair and scalp, it alleviates oiliness and dandruff. As an inhalation, this oil soothes the nerves, relieves stress, and fights insomnia. It is also a powerful aphrodisiac.

Personal/Spiritual Growth: Patchouli essential oil balances the mind, body, and spirit. It also helps us navigate around obstacles so we can take steps to achieve our goals. Use during meditation to quiet the mind and ground and center spiritual awareness in the body. Add to bathwater to ease mental exhaustion and emotional stress. With massage, this oil boosts sexual energy.

Pine

ORIGINS

Pine essential oil comes from the needles of the coniferous tree *Pinus sylvestris*, also called Scots pine. These trees are widely cultivated for ornamental use as well as for their timber and resinous sap, used to make turpentine and pine tar. With its invigorating, woodsy scent, this oil has therapeutic, medicinal, and household cleaning uses.

HISTORY/LORE

Native to Europe and Asia, the pine tree became a popular Christmas tree choice in the United States in the 1950s, despite the fact that it does not grow well in many areas of the country due to climate and soil differences. The Native Americans chewed pine needles to treat scurvy; chewing releases the oil, which is rich in vitamin C. Stuffing a mattress with pine needles helps keep lice and fleas at bay.

USES

Healing Uses: Pine essential oil has many of the same properties as eucalyptus (see entry in this chapter). Used in massage or bathwater, it soothes sore muscles and joints. As an inhalation, it treats respiratory problems, acting as an expectorant to clear congestion. It is also an effective stimulant, boosting metabolism and increasing energy levels.

Personal/Spiritual Growth: Pine essential oil clears and refreshes the mind and grounds the body. It balances the heart and sacral chakras, fostering inner peace and self-love. The powerful scent moves the spirit while allowing for acceptance and the acknowledgment of inner wisdom. Meditate with this oil to lift a dark mood and enhance spiritual focus.

Rosemary

ORIGINS

Rosemary essential oil comes from the leaves of the herb discussed in Chapter 2. The word *rosemary* comes from the Latin *ros marinus*: *ros*, meaning "dew"—perhaps from the oil glands on the undersides of the leaves—and *marinus*, meaning "of the sea." This oil has a strong, herbaceous fragrance.

HISTORY/LORE

Rosemary essential oil is a staple in traditional Indian medicine. Before refrigeration, this herb was often used as a food preservative. It is said that inhaling the scent of rosemary essential oil brings back long-forgotten memories. The Swiss German physician and botanist Paracelsus (1493–1541) valued rosemary oil for its powerful healing abilities.

USES

Healing Uses: Applied topically, rosemary essential oil stimulates hair growth, conditions the scalp and hair, and treats dandruff and split ends. It also benefits the skin, particularly in cases of acne and eczema. This oil supports digestion and relieves stomach cramps, constipation, and bloating. With massage, it soothes sore muscles.

Personal/Spiritual Growth:
Rosemary essential oil overcomes fatigue and rejuvenates the mind. It brings clarity, renews enthusiasm, and inspires creativity. This oil will restore your passion for life and help you follow your true path. It also serves to remind us that we are spiritual beings and that there is more to life than what is seen.

Sandalwood

ORIGINS

Sandalwood essential oil comes from the fragrant inner heartwood of trees of the genus *Santalum*, particularly Indian sandalwood (*Santalum album*) and Australian sandalwood (*Santalum spicatum*). This oil has a warm, woody aroma—the Australian variety is milder than the Indian.

HISTORY/LORE

It takes forty years for an Indian sandalwood tree to reach maturity and produce essential oil of the highest potency. Due to illegal logging, there is currently a shortage of Indian sandalwood trees, which has caused Australian sandalwood to become more prevalent on the market. Both varieties have a long history of use as incense, perfume, and medicine.

USES

Healing Uses: Sandalwood essential oil is high in sesquiterpenes, natural compounds that stimulate the limbic system of the brain. This is the area of the brain that controls breathing, heart rate, blood pressure, memory, stress levels, and hormone balance. This oil has an overall relaxing effect, making it an excellent sleep remedy. It also has antiseptic, anti-inflammatory, and astringent qualities.

Personal/Spiritual Growth: This essential oil warms the heart and fortifies the inner self. It assists in overcoming vulnerability and emotional challenges. Working with the root and sacral chakras, this oil facilitates grounding and increases confidence and sensuality. This is an excellent essential oil for meditation, as it encourages quiet focus and brings the attention inward.

Tea Tree

ORIGINS

Tea tree essential oil comes from the leaves of the melaleuca tree (*Melaleuca alternifolia*), which is native to Australia. Also called melaleuca oil, this essential oil has a fresh, medicinal aroma.

HISTORY/LORE

The discovery of the melaleuca tree is commonly attributed to the British explorer Captain James Cook (1728–1779) and his sailors, who brewed an infusion using the tree's leaves to fight scurvy; hence the name "tea tree." However, the indigenous Australian Aborigines were using the leaves to treat headaches and respiratory problems long before Cook arrived.

USES

Healing Uses: Tea tree essential oil is excellent for the skin and can be applied topically to treat acne, wounds, burns, infections, and insect bites. It also has antiviral properties, making it an effective treatment for colds and flu. As an inhalation, it acts as a stimulant, increasing circulation and boosting the immune system. Used during massage, this oil soothes muscular aches.

Personal/Spiritual Growth: This essential oil boosts energy and renews optimism and self-confidence. It stimulates the mind as well as the body, sharpening focus and refreshing thought processes. Tea tree essential oil helps to heal emotional wounds, releasing feelings of distrust, guilt, and shame. Add to an amulet to bring strength.

Vanilla

ORIGINS

Vanilla essential oil is derived from the dried brown pods of *Vanilla planifolia*, a climbing vine with trumpet-shaped white flowers related to the orchid. Because this oil is extracted using a solvent, it is technically an absolute, not an essential oil. It has a sweet, balsamic scent.

HISTORY/LORE

The Totonac people of the eastern coastal and mountainous regions of Mexico were the first to cultivate vanilla and were the world's main vanilla producers until the mid-nineteenth century. The Spanish explorers who arrived in Mexico in the early sixteenth century gave the plant its name: The Spanish *vainilla* is a diminutive of *vaina*, meaning "sheath"—a reference to the shape of the seedpod.

USES

Healing Uses: Vanilla absolute is calming and comforting. It has a general relaxing effect on the mind and body and is commonly used to relieve stress, tension, anxiety, and panic attacks. It also has antidepressant qualities. Used in massage, vanilla absolute is a powerful aphrodisiac.

Personal/Spiritual Growth: This warming absolute dissolves anger and frustration, relaxes the mind, and fosters a sense of inner peace. It stimulates the sacral chakra, boosting self-confidence and encouraging intimacy. It also has a very sensual quality; use with a partner to deepen physical connection. In meditation, it brings the spirit into balance.

Ylang-Ylang

ORIGINS

Ylang-ylang essential oil comes from the fragrant flowers of the tropical Asian tree *Cananga odorata*. It is native to the Philippines and Indonesia, but it is also grown in Polynesia, Melanesia, Micronesia, and the Comoro Islands. The oil has a sweet, floral scent.

HISTORY/LORE

In Indonesia, ylang-ylang flower petals are strewn on the beds of newlywed couples. In the Philippines, ylang-ylang flowers are used to adorn religious figures, and women wear strings of the flowers around their necks. Ylang-ylang oil is a main ingredient in the famous perfume Chanel No. 5.

USES

Healing Uses: Ylang-ylang essential oil is very calming and relaxing, making it effective for treating stress-related high blood pressure. It also relieves depression and sleeplessness. Applied topically, this oil benefits the skin and supports hair growth. Added to bathwater, it soothes symptoms of PMS and menopause, including irritability and mood swings.

Personal/Spiritual Growth: This essential oil is perfect for those who have trouble forgiving or being kind to themselves. It aids in releasing negative emotions such as anger and fear and boosts positive emotions, self-esteem, and spiritual awareness. Ylang-ylang works with the heart chakra to increase self-love. It also encourages harmony by balancing male and female energies in the body.

5

The Power of Fire and Light

It's difficult to overstate the impact of fire on human life. From light and heat to cooking and cultural traditions, fire plays a central role in almost everything we do. In fact, some believe that it is the use of fire that actually makes us human. Several years ago, the British primatologist Richard Wrangham proposed his "cooking hypothesis" to explain our evolution from bipedal apes into modern human beings. His hypothesis states that the use of fire is responsible for the relatively speedy development of *Homo erectus*, which emerged just 500,000 years after *Homo habilis*, the first creature generally considered to be human. Wrangham argues that once our predecessors started cooking food, it sped up the process of evolution, leading to smaller teeth, a smaller digestive tract, and a larger brain.

Archaeologists have not yet discovered evidence that proves Wrangham's hypothesis, but they recently came closer than ever before. In 2012, a team of archaeologists discovered traces of a million-year-old campfire in South Africa's Wonderwerk Cave. Prior to this, the earliest evidence of human-controlled fire was a series of hearths found in Israel dating to between 690,000 and 790,000 years ago.

Regardless of whether the use of fire directly contributed to the development of human beings as they exist today, there is no doubt that fire is one of the most important elements in our lives. In this chapter, you'll discover various ways of harnessing fire and light to benefit your mind, body, and spirit.

Candles

ORIGINS

There's not much to a candle—just a solid mass of tallow, wax, or another fatty substance with a wick running through the center that is burned to provide light. But these simple objects come in all shapes and sizes, from pillars to tapers to votives, and there are seemingly countless applications for candles in cultural, religious, and other traditions. They are also used in various healing methods, including candle therapy, aromatherapy, and color therapy (see entry in this chapter). The word *candle* comes from the Latin *candere*, meaning "to shine."

HISTORY/LORE

The ancient Egyptians are believed to have been the first to make and use candles, although their candles did not have wicks and were instead more like torches, made of reeds dipped in melted tallow (animal fat). The Romans are credited with being the first to use wicked candles, which they made by dipping rolled papyrus in melted tallow or beeswax. Wicked candles were also used in ancient China, Japan, and India. Hanukkah, the Jewish holiday that centers on the lighting of candles, dates back to the second century B.C.E.

USES

In addition to providing light, candles have been used throughout history in spiritual ceremonies and traditions as well as for healing and therapeutic purposes. Candle therapy is a practice that unites the body, mind, and spirit. Focusing or meditating on a flame has a relaxing effect that has been shown to reduce stress and can even improve conditions such as high blood pressure. Scented candles may be especially effective in these practices. You can also buy unscented candles and add your own scents to them using flower essences or essential oils (see Chapters 3 and 4). In the magical realm, candles are often used in spells, rituals, visualizations, and more. Another fun activity is to try making your own candles at home. In addition to personal use, they make great gifts!

Incense

ORIGINS

Incense is a natural substance, often combined with essential oils, that releases an aromatic smoke when burned. There are two main types: combustible (or direct-burning), which burns on its own, and non-combustible (or indirect-burning),

which requires a separate heat source. The most common form of combustible incense is paste formed around a bamboo stick, but it may also be paste formed into a cone shape. Both forms are lit and then the flame is blown out, allowing the resulting ember to smolder. Non-combustible incense is usually in whole, powdered, or paste form and heated on charcoal or in a container over a flame or coals. The word *incense* comes from the Latin verb *incendere*, which means "to set on fire."

HISTORY/LORE

The ancient Egyptians burned resins as incense for their pleasant scent and also incorporated them into their ceremonial and embalming processes. The ancient Greeks and Romans also burned resins as incense and used them during cremations. Frankincense and myrrh (see entries in Chapter 4) were among the first resins burned as incense, and aromatic herbs and spices also have been used throughout history for this purpose. The Chinese have been burning items such as cinnamon and sandalwood as incense since as far back as 2000 B.C.E.

USES

There are many reasons to burn incense, but perhaps the simplest is that it smells good. You may burn incense to counteract a foul odor or to refresh the air in an unventilated area or sickroom. Many believe that the smoke of incense can also clear away negative energies, making way for new, positive energy. For this reason, it is recommended that you burn incense in a new home to remove any negative influences from the previous owners. Rosemary, sage, and thyme are favorites for cleansing and purifying a space. Incense burning is also a great accompaniment to meditation—frankincense and sandalwood are excellent for this. Often incense will be made up of two or more ingredients; for example, the Indian incense nag champa contains frangipani and sandalwood. Incense may also be incorporated into magic spells, rituals, and other practices.

Holders

ORIGINS

Now that you know all about candles and incense, you may be wondering how to physically incorporate them into your home. After all, a burning candle or stick of incense can't just be placed on the table and left unattended. Luckily there are all sorts of holders, tools, and other products that will help you enjoy the flickering flames and smoky scents without fear of setting the house on fire. These include candlesticks, lanterns, jars, sconces, censers, and incense burners.

HISTORY/LORE

Archaeologists have found incense burners dating back to 3000 B.C.E. The ancient Chinese, Japanese, and Mesoamerican civilizations all used censers (vessels for burning incense), and censers also appear in the traditions of religious institutions such as the Eastern Orthodox Church and the Roman Catholic Church. The menorah, a nine-branched candelabrum used in celebration of the Jewish holiday Hanukkah, is one of the most historically and culturally significant candleholders. There is one candle for each night of Hanukkah, plus a shamash or "servant candle," which is used to light the other eight.

USES

If you've ever gone camping, you are probably well acquainted with the lantern, a portable case, usually with transparent sides, for holding and protecting a light—historically a candle but nowadays an electric light is usually substituted. In the home, almost any type of holder may be used to display a candle. Candles are commonly displayed in candlesticks on the table to create ambience while dining, and jars, sconces, and other holders may be used around the home. Incense burners range from the simple to the complex. An ash catcher or boat burner is typically a strip of wood that catches ashes as they fall from an incense stick. The most common form of burner for cone incense is the brass burner—a small brass bowl with a lid. Loose incense burners are essentially little charcoal grills, with a divider between the burning coals and the incense, or a simple bowl of sand upon which the burning charcoal is placed.

Light Therapy

ORIGINS

Light therapy, also known as phototherapy, is a treatment that consists of exposure to daylight or artificial light. It is often prescribed in cases of seasonal affective disorder (SAD), non-seasonal depression, delayed sleep-phase disorder, and certain skin conditions, including psoriasis, eczema, neonatal jaundice, and even skin cancer.

HISTORY/LORE

Light therapy, once called heliotherapy, is not a new idea. The ancient Egyptians discovered that exposure to the sun could disinfect and prevent disease. The ancient Greeks built structures called solaria for sunbathing, with the purpose of treating skin ailments and increasing health and vitality. The Incas of Peru worshipped the sun god, Inti, and had many ceremonies and rituals based around the sun. In India, the solar deity Surya is important in the Hindu religion, and worship includes a series of "sun salutations" performed at dawn.

USES

Those who suffer from the winter blues may actually have seasonal affective disorder (SAD), a mood disorder caused by lack of exposure to sunlight and characterized by low energy and symptoms of depression, such as sleeping too much. Even if getting outdoors is not an option, you can use an artificial light box indoors to "cheer up" your brain. This treatment may also help sufferers of non-seasonal depression. Those with delayed sleep-phase disorder typically don't fall asleep until the early hours of the morning, and then they are too tired to wake up for school or work. Light therapy upon awakening has been shown to advance one's sleep phase; this is often done in combination with light restriction in the evening. While artificial light boxes designed for these conditions filter out UV light, light therapy treatments for certain skin conditions require UV light to be effective. In these cases, the light exposure slows down cell growth and inhibits inflammation that causes conditions like psoriasis and eczema.

Color Therapy

ORIGINS

Color therapy, also called chromotherapy, is an alternative healing method that uses colored light to balance the energies of the body. Although color therapy is not a widely used practice, it is gaining popularity in the holistic and natural therapy realms with patients suffering from depression, those recovering from stroke, and others. Tools used in color therapy may include lamps, candles, gemstones, crystal or glass prisms, and colored eye lenses.

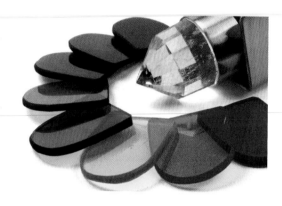

HISTORY/LORE

The use of color therapy goes all the way back to the ancient Egyptians and Greeks, who used colored stones and crystals for healing purposes. The Persian philosopher and scientist Avicenna (980–1037) wrote extensively about the importance of color in medical diagnosis and treatment. He believed that red increased circulation, blue slowed the blood, and yellow reduced pain and inflammation. In the Hindu, yogic, and other traditions, each of the chakras, or energy centers in the body, corresponds with a different color: The root chakra is red, the sacral or base chakra is orange, the solar plexus or navel chakra is yellow, the heart chakra is green, the throat chakra is blue, the third-eye chakra is indigo, and the crown chakra is violet.

USES

Color therapy has been shown to be an effective treatment for a wide range of illnesses and conditions. Blue light is used to treat neonatal jaundice. Exposure to white light benefits those who suffer from seasonal affective disorder (SAD). In athletes, red light is shown to provide quick bursts of energy, while blue light assists with steadier energy needs. Pink light has a tranquilizing effect and can be used to calm aggression, hostility, or anxiety. Yellow stimulates the mind and body and can benefit those dealing with depression. If you think you might benefit from color therapy, you can purchase one of many products on the market designed for this purpose, or you can seek treatment with a practitioner who incorporates color therapy methods into his or her practice.

6

The Power of Sound

Our modern lives are extremely noisy. From the rumble of passing traffic to the hum of heating and cooling systems to the audio pumping out of our televisions, stereos, and computers, we rarely have the luxury of focusing on just one sound—let alone complete peace and quiet. For most of us, it's difficult to remember a time before all the noise, and perhaps we've grown so accustomed to it that we don't even notice it anymore. But whether or not we're aware of it, all those competing sounds can clog our minds and prevent us from achieving deep focus and relaxation.

For contrast, let's go back for a moment to the beginning of human history, a time before highways and electricity and the Internet. Back then, the only sounds to be heard were the sounds of nature—wind in the trees, a rushing stream, insects and animals and fellow human beings. Musical instruments and song are just about as old as humanity itself, so throw those in there, too. Now imagine a world with just these sounds. Peaceful, isn't it?

This chapter is all about the power of sound to transport you to a quieter, simpler time, or perhaps deeper inside your own mind. The instruments and practices discussed in these pages have long histories and multiple applications in various spiritual traditions. Perhaps you'd like to add chanting to your yoga practice or incorporate flute music into your meditation routine. Maybe you'll even try your hand at learning a new instrument or join a group activity such as a drum circle. However you choose to experiment with these powerful sounds, they will surely open up a new dimension in your life.

Bell

ORIGINS

A bell is a hollow musical instrument that produces a ringing tone when struck. It is usually made of metal, but it may also be ceramic, glass, or another material. A bell is typically cup-shaped with a flared opening, and the striking implement may be a "tongue" inside the bell or a separate mallet or hammer used on the outside of the bell. Tubular bells, or chimes, are a common variation. Bells are often associated with religion and spirituality, but they may also be used in healing and other practices.

HISTORY/LORE

The earliest evidence of bells dates back to the third millennium B.C.E. in Neolithic China. These pottery bells were replaced with metal bells about 1,000 years later. Bells have long played a prominent role in both eastern and western religions, including Buddhism, Hinduism, and Christianity. Historically, they have been used as church bells that call worshipers to services, as instruments used in musical performances, and as tools in agricultural and domestic labor, either to help keep track of animals or to call workers in from the fields. The largest existing bell, the Tsar Bell, weighs 222 U.S. tons and is on display in Moscow's Kremlin Museum. The most significant bell in American history, the Liberty Bell, which was rung in July 1776 to mark America's independence from Britain, is located in Philadelphia.

USES

Bells have many musical and practical uses, but in the New Age realm, bells are often incorporated into spiritual practices. For example, in meditation, the sound of a bell may help keep your mind focused in the present instead of wandering off into the past or the future. This is often an option in group meditation, but if you are meditating alone, you can try listening to a recording of bells during your practice. In magical practices, bells may be used to summon spirits, or to mark the beginning or end of a ceremony or ritual.

Chanting

ORIGINS

Chanting is a practice similar to singing except instead of using your full vocal range you use a limited range of notes or even just one note. Chanting is common in many religious traditions as well as in spiritual practices such as yoga and meditation. Chants are also used in recreational settings, such as sports events and music performances. The word *chant* comes from the Latin *cantare*, meaning "to sing."

HISTORY/LORE

Although the exact origin of the practice of chanting is unknown, it has long been a prominent part of many of the world's most ancient religions, including Buddhism, Christianity, Hinduism, Islam, and Judaism. In Buddhism, chanting is a way of preparing the mind for meditation. Gregorian chant, named for Pope Gregory I (c. 540–604) and traditionally sung by church choirs, is practiced in the Roman Catholic religion. Both Hinduism and Islam include the practice of chanting mantras (see entry in this chapter). In Judaism, portions of the Torah are often chanted during services.

USES

Perhaps you are already familiar with chanting as part of the practice of your religion, or you may have been introduced to chanting at a yoga class or meditation retreat. If you've never chanted before, don't worry. It can feel a bit awkward the first time you try it, but before long you'll be basking in the many benefits of this ancient practice. In meditation, chanting turns the mind inward and allows you to stay present, focus on the sound of your voice and your breath, and begin a process of self-observation and discovery. Chanting at the beginning of a yoga class is a great way to prepare your mind for what you're about to experience and to stay present in your body. The vibration and sound can also help you push through any mental, emotional, or physical barriers. When chanting in any kind of group setting, you'll find that the practice serves to unite those present and create a feeling of "oneness."

Drum

ORIGINS

A drum is a percussion instrument consisting of a hollow cylindrical shell with a membrane (also called a drumhead or drum skin) stretched over one or both ends. A sound is produced when the membrane is struck with the hand, a stick, a mallet, or another implement. The word *drum* is most likely of imitative origin, or onomatopoeia, meaning that the sound of the word is meant to imitate the sound associated with the object. Drums have many musical, ceremonial, spiritual, and military applications.

HISTORY/LORE

The drum is one of the world's oldest musical instruments, dating back to 6000 B.C.E. in Mesopotamia. The ancient Greeks and Romans used a shallow circular drum called a tympanum in worship ceremonies. The "talking drum" of West Africa, whose tone can be regulated to mimic human speech, has been in use for 2,500 years. The drum kit—a collection of multiple drums played together—first appeared toward the end of the nineteenth century. Throughout history, drums have been used for military purposes, such as to rally troops or intimidate the enemy.

USES

In addition to enjoying the sound of drums in music, you may also consider incorporating drums into your spiritual practices. For example, shamanic drumming induces a trance-like state with the purpose of connecting with the spiritual dimension of existence. It typically starts out with a slow rhythm that steadily increases and then slows again at the end of the session. You might try listening to a recording of drums during meditation, or perhaps join a local drum circle to get in on the action and experience the unifying powers of this ancient instrument.

Flute

ORIGINS

A flute is a high-pitched woodwind instrument that consists of a slender tube that is closed at one end and has keys and finger holes on one side. Sound is produced when breath is blown into an opening near the closed end. The oldest known flutes are made of bone or ivory; more modern flutes are made of wood or metal. A person who plays the flute is called a flautist.

HISTORY/LORE

The world's oldest known musical instruments are flutes made of bird bone and mammoth ivory. Discovered in caves in southwestern Germany, these flutes are estimated to be between 42,000 and 43,000 years old. Flutes have been central to Indian classical music since 1500 B.C.E. The Hindu deity Krishna is typically depicted playing the flute. The German inventor and musician Theobald Boehm (1794–1881) is essentially responsible for the flute as we know it today. His system of flute keywork is known as the Boehm system.

USES

Flute music is considered very relaxing, which makes it a popular choice for meditation and other spiritual practices. Tibetan flute music is wonderful for meditation, particularly Zen Buddhist meditation, as it produces a deep sense of inner calm and well-being. Chinese bamboo flute music is another great option for your spiritual practice. If you are looking to take up a new hobby, you might also enjoy playing the flute yourself! Its focus on breathwork is actually quite meditative. (See the entry on breathwork in Chapter 9 to learn more about this.)

Gong

ORIGINS

A gong is a musical instrument that consists of a metal (usually bronze) disk that makes a loud, resonant sound when struck with a padded mallet or hammer. The disk generally has a rim and either is flat or has a raised knob called a "boss" or "nipple" in the center. Gongs are usually suspended vertically from a cord, although there are also gongs that are played horizontally, such as bowl gongs.

HISTORY/LORE

The gong originated in China and later spread to Southeast Asia and Africa. Ancient gongs had many uses, including calling workers in from the fields, announcing military presence, and aiding in meditation and ceremonial practices. Gongs are prominently featured in gamelans, which are Indonesian orchestras composed entirely of percussion instruments. Sculptural gongs serve as both a musical instrument and a piece of art.

USES

The sound of a gong adds a new dimension to meditation and other spiritual practices. The tone keeps your mind focused in the present and, depending on the size of the gong, the vibration can sometimes be felt physically, bringing awareness back to the body. One very popular New Age practice is the gong bath. This is a form of sound therapy in which a gong master plays a gong in the center of a room while "bathers" lie on the ground around the gong and soak up the sound and vibration. It's best to do this in a private or group setting with an actual gong so you can "feel" its power, but you can also try it at home with recorded gong sounds.

Mantra

ORIGINS

A mantra is a sound, word, or phrase that is repeated mentally or aloud as part of a spiritual or other practice. It is believed that the use of a mantra can have a powerful or even life-changing effect. In Hinduism, mantras are considered sacred. The word *mantra* comes from the Sanskrit *mantrah*, meaning "counsel," "prayer," or "hymn."

HISTORY/LORE

Mantras are a major component of the Vedas, a body of ancient Indian texts composed in Sanskrit. Dating back to roughly 1500 B.C.E., the Vedas are the oldest Hindu texts and among the oldest sacred texts in the world. In Hinduism, mantras accompany ritual acts. In Buddhism, mantras are chanted in meditation and to achieve enlightenment. Perhaps the simplest and best-known mantra is "Om," which is known as the "pranava mantra," or the supreme mantra. (In Sanskrit, *prana* means "life force.") Many yoga classes open and close with the chanting of this mantra.

USES

A mantra can serve various purposes in your spiritual practice. Starting off a meditation or yoga session with the chanting of a mantra can help you state your intention for the session and keep your mind focused throughout. You might also choose to use a motivational mantra for times during your practice where you feel stuck or uninspired. Even something as simple as "I can do this" can help get you through tough times in a spiritual practice or in daily life. A mantra can also be a sort of prayer—to a deity, nature, the universe, or yourself. You can use an established Hindu, Buddhist, or other mantra, or you can make up your own.

Rattle

ORIGINS

A rattle is a hollow percussion instrument that makes a sound when
shaken. It can be made of almost
any material and contains tiny items such as seeds, beans, or pebbles that make
the rattling sound. The word *rattle* is most likely of imitative origin, or onomatopoeia, meaning that the sound of the word is meant to imitate the sound associated with the object. Etymologically, it comes from the Old English *hratele*,
a kind of plant with rattling seed capsules.

HISTORY/LORE

The rattle is one of the oldest musical instruments. It comes in many different
forms, from the maraca, a Latin American instrument that consists of a dried
hollow gourd traditionally played in pairs, to the egg shaker, which is small and
egg-shaped. Native Americans use wood, rawhide, gourds, and other materials to
make rattles used in tribal dances and ceremonies. Shamans of northern Asia and
North and South America use rattles for healing, divination, and communication
with spirits. The rattlesnake has a natural rattle at the end of its tail to warn away
predators. However, this is not a true rattle, as there is nothing inside the tail that
is causing the sound. Instead, the sound is emitted when the various "buttons"
or segments of the tail vibrate against one another. These segments develop
throughout the snake's life as it repeatedly sheds its skin.

USES

Rattles aren't just for babies, although they do help infants develop cognitive and motor skills. Adults can also benefit from the power of the rattle.
In meditation, the sound of a rattle has a similar effect to that of a drum or
a gong (see entries in this chapter): It focuses your attention and keeps you
grounded in the present moment. You might also try using a rattle in the
shamanic tradition of calling upon spirits for aid during a struggle.

Singing Bowl

ORIGINS

A singing bowl is a percussion instrument that is actually a type of standing bell. The bowl produces a sound when struck with a mallet or other implement, or when the implement is rubbed along the rim of the bowl. The resonant sound is reminiscent of singing; hence the name. Singing bowls are most often metal, usually a copper-heavy alloy, but may also be made of quartz crystal.

HISTORY/LORE

The singing bowl originated in the Himalayan regions of Tibet, Nepal, and India and is now used worldwide. Traditionally, singing bowls were made of a combination of seven metals corresponding to the seven "planets" that were known at the time: gold (the sun), silver (the moon), copper (Venus), iron (Mars), tin (Jupiter), mercury/quicksilver (Mercury), and lead (Saturn). There is also a connection to the seven chakras, or energy centers, of the body. In some Buddhist practices, the sound of the singing bowl signals the beginning and end of a period of silent meditation. In Japan, singing bowls are used in funeral ceremonies.

USES

Singing bowls are used in many spiritual and holistic health traditions for relaxation, meditation, and healing. You can meditate on the sound of the bowl itself or you can use the sound as a way to focus your attention on the present moment. The singing bowl is sometimes used at the end of a yoga practice during shavasana, or corpse pose, to aid in relaxation following a strenuous session. Singing bowls are available for purchase in most New Age stores as well as online.

Tuning Fork

ORIGINS

A tuning fork is a two-pronged metal (usually steel) device that is used to tune a musical instrument. When struck, it resonates at a specific, constant pitch based on the length and mass of the two prongs. The longer the prongs, the lower the tone. The tuning fork is also used as a musical instrument in its own right and has been used in medicine to diagnose hearing impairments.

HISTORY/LORE

The British trumpeter John Shore (c. 1662–1752) invented the tuning fork in 1711. Prior to this invention, wooden pitch pipes were used, but their vulnerability to temperature and humidity made them unreliable. The American physicist Albert Michelson (1852–1931) used the tuning fork in his groundbreaking work on measuring the speed of light. Beginning in the 1960s, tiny quartz crystal tuning forks have been used as the timekeeping elements in some clocks and watches. These timepieces kept much better time than their balance-wheel predecessors.

USES

In addition to its musical and timekeeping applications, the tuning fork is used in a wide variety of healing methods and spiritual practices, including massage, meditation, hypnosis, Reiki, and yoga. The resonant tone and vibration induce a state of relaxation, relieving stress and bringing mental clarity. For healing purposes, you simply strike the tuning fork and then place it near the affected area. You can also do this with any chakras, or energy centers of the body, that need balancing. For best results with tuning fork healing, seek the guidance of a professional.

Wind Chimes

ORIGINS

A wind chime is an arrangement of suspended tubes, rods, or bells spaced close together so that when the wind blows they collide and produce a jingling sound. Wind chimes may be almost any material but are most often glass, wood, metal, or ceramic. They are typically hung outside the home, in the garden, or in another location where they can be enjoyed both visually and aurally. The word *chime* derives from the word *cymbal*, which comes from the Greek *kumbe*, meaning "bowl."

HISTORY/LORE

The earliest evidence of wind chimes, found in Southeast Asia, dates back to roughly 3000 B.C.E. Made of bone, wood, or bamboo, these early wind chimes were used to ward off evil spirits. Wind chimes are also a fundamental part of the ancient Chinese practice of feng shui and are thought to support the flow of chi, or universal energy.

USES

The simplest use of a wind chime is for relaxation. The pleasant jingling sound can calm and focus the mind, reduce stress, and bring clarity. You might also find this helpful during practices like yoga and meditation. If you don't have a wind chime of your own, you can use a recording of wind chimes; there are many available online. For feng shui use, be sure to revisit the bagua in the Introduction of this book to match the material of your wind chime to the appropriate sector of the home. For example, metal is associated with the western area or the Children/Creativity sector, while wood is the element for the eastern area or the Family/Foundation sector.

7

THE POWER OF INSIGHT:
Divination Systems, Tools, and Practices

The New Age items and practices in this book have a wide range of uses and applications, and come from cultural traditions that may have originated thousands of years and thousands of miles apart. But what they all have in common is a connection to something outside the realm of the visible world. Tapping into the unseen forces of the universe requires an open mind, an open heart, and a sense of adventure, and nowhere is this more important than in the area of divination.

Divination is the practice of foretelling future events through supernatural means. If you thought crystal balls only appeared in children's stories about wizards, think again! Not all of the systems, tools, and practices in this chapter deal specifically with telling the future, but they are all means of gleaning information that cannot be observed with the naked eye—or any of the other four senses. From searching the stars for information about the events in our lives (astrology) to searching our dreams for important messages (dream interpretation), the topics covered in this chapter add a new dimension to our daily lives and show us that perhaps there's more to life than meets the eye.

Astral Projection

ORIGINS

Astral projection, or astral travel, is a type of out-of-body experience in which the astral body leaves the physical body and travels in a separate dimension known as the astral plane or spirit world. The astral body is a supersensible body, meaning it is beyond or above perception by the physical senses. Many people believe there is a silver cord that connects the two bodies during astral projection, which allows the traveler to return to his or her physical body when the experience ends. Some believe that dreaming is a form of astral projection.

HISTORY/LORE

The exact origins of the practice of astral projection are unknown. What is clear, though, is that the idea of astral travel is rooted in the ancient religious belief in an afterlife. In many religions, it is believed that when the physical body dies, the spirit or soul continues on or ascends to a higher realm. The ancient Egyptians believed the soul had the ability to hover outside the physical body. The ancient Indian religions of Hinduism and Buddhism include a belief in reincarnation, which is the rebirth of the soul (or spirit or consciousness) in another body after death.

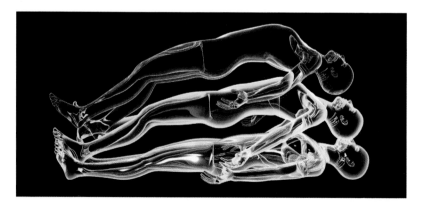

USES

In the New Age world, it is generally believed that astral projection is a skill you can learn, like swimming or riding a bike. It simply takes practice. Most astral travel practices look a lot like meditation: You find a comfortable position in a quiet place, close your eyes, and achieve a state of complete relaxation and focus. From there, your mind does the work of moving your soul from your body. But why would you want to do this in the first place? There are many reasons, but perhaps the most compelling is that we are mortal creatures. No matter what we do, our physical bodies will age and eventually fail. Thinking about our mortality can cause immense fear, grief, and sadness. But what if there were more to us than what we see in the mirror? The idea of an astral body and a life beyond the physical world brings many people a feeling of peace. It also helps in dealing with the loss of loved ones. Astral projection is a way of getting in touch with our non-physical selves and learning about who we are on the deepest level.

Astrology

ORIGINS

Astrology is the study of the sun, moon, stars, and planets based on the premise that there is a connection between these celestial bodies and the events that happen here on Earth. A major component of astrology is the zodiac—the band of sky demarcated by the path the sun takes as it travels around the Earth over the course of a year. In Western astrology, the twelve signs of the zodiac—Aries, Taurus,

Gemini, Cancer, Leo, Virgo, Libra, Scorpio, Sagittarius, Capricorn, Aquarius, and Pisces—are used to generate one's horoscope, a forecast of a person's future based on the position of the stars and planets on a given day, usually the person's birthday. But there are many other forms of astrology, some going back thousands of years. Chinese astrology also includes a zodiac that is divided into twelve parts, but in this case it represents twelve years, not twelve months. Each year in the Chinese zodiac is represented by a different animal. Vedic astrology is the traditional Hindu system of astrology. Its Indian name, *Jyotish*, means "science of light," referring to the idea that the celestial bodies shine their light and energy upon the Earth.

HISTORY/LORE

The Babylonians are generally credited with the creation of astrology—although it is believed that they adopted the idea of the zodiac from the ancient Egyptians. Early on, astrology was largely used to predict weather patterns for agricultural purposes, but over time the practice broadened to include forecasting natural disasters, war, and other events that affected human life. Greek philosophers such as Plato and Aristotle studied astrology and contributed to it being considered a science. However, the two related fields of astrology and astronomy eventually diverged, and today astrology is generally considered a pseudoscience.

USES

There are many ways to incorporate astrology into your life. The horoscopes you find in magazines and newspapers can be fun to read, but they're not always based on true astrology. If you really want to get into the study of astrology, there is a wealth of resources out there—from books and websites to professional astrologers—to help you get started. A fun first step is to go online and get a copy of your birth chart, a diagram that depicts the positions of the celestial bodies at the moment when you were born.

Aura Reading

ORIGINS

An aura is a field of energy surrounding a person or object. Some believe that the ability to see auras can be learned and honed with practice; others believe that only certain people are endowed with this skill or "gift." In an aura reading, a psychic, healer, or other specialist examines your aura for information about your thoughts, feelings, and other personal attributes. Sometimes auras appear as layers of colored light surrounding a person. Other times auras are invisible but can still be sensed or perceived by the specialist. The word *aura* comes from the Greek *aura*, meaning "breath."

HISTORY/LORE

The concept of auras is ancient and is found in many spiritual traditions. In the Bible, references to light surrounding certain figures are often interpreted as references to auras. Many depictions of Jesus, Mary, and other biblical figures include shining halos or radiant layers of light surrounding their bodies. In Hinduism, the colors of a person's aura are considered to be kundalini energy, which resides at the base of the spine until it is activated (through practices such as yoga) and propelled upward through the chakras. The colors of the Buddhist flag (blue, yellow, red, white, and orange) represent the colors of the aura that surrounded the Buddha when he achieved enlightenment.

USES

Like a palm reading or a tarot card reading (see entries in this chapter), an aura reading can be a fun and interesting way to learn more about yourself. Of course, the success of an aura reading has a lot to do with the skill and experience of the specialist you visit. Find a well-respected aura reader in your area or solicit a suggestion from someone you trust. Also, make sure you go into the experience with an open mind. A good time to get an aura reading is when you are at a crossroads in your life, are uncertain about your feelings on a certain matter, or have questions about something you're experiencing. Some aura readers will discuss your past and future as well as your present, while others will only evaluate your aura in the present moment.

Biorhythms

ORIGINS

Biorhythms are rhythmic biological cycles that affect our physical, emotional, and intellectual activity. Many believe that by charting these biorhythms mathematically we can predict our level of activity in each of these areas. Most biorhythm models use three cycles: a twenty-three-day physical cycle, a twenty-eight-day emotional cycle, and a thirty-three-day intellectual cycle. The idea is that by monitoring the highs and lows of these cycles, you can improve your life. For example, you might try to avoid having difficult conversations with your partner during emotional lows, or you might wait until a time of physical highs to engage in an athletic competition.

HISTORY/LORE

One of the first people to study biorhythms was the German physician Wilhelm Fliess (1858–1928), a close friend of Sigmund Freud. He labeled the twenty-three-day cycle "male" and the twenty-eight-day cycle "female," the latter due to its connection to the female menstrual cycle. Charting biorhythms became a popular practice in the 1970s, in part because of a series of books by Bernard Gittelson, including *Biorhythm: A Personal Science*. At the time, it was common to see biorhythm machines in video arcades and biorhythm charts alongside horoscopes in newspapers. You could even buy your own personal hand-held biorhythm calculator, such as the Casio Biolator.

USES

Biorhythm theory is not as popular as it once was, but there are still many people who chart their biorhythms and many physical and mental health practitioners who chart the biorhythms of their patients with the goal of improving overall health or treating certain conditions, such as sleep disorders or depression. The simplest way to get started with biorhythms on your own is to try one of the many biorhythms calculators that are available online, most of which can generate your biorhythms chart based on your date of birth.

Book of Shadows

ORIGINS

A book of shadows is an important text in the Neopagan religion of Wicca containing religious texts and instructions for magical rituals and spells. When books of shadows first appeared, there was only one book per coven (group of witches), kept by the high priest or priestess, but nowadays it is common for each witch to have his or her own copy. Today, a book of shadows often resembles a journal, with personal thoughts and reflections on one's magical experiences in addition to more formal texts, recipes, and instructions.

HISTORY/LORE

The British Wiccan Gerald Gardner (1884–1964), widely regarded as the "father of Wicca," is credited with creating the first book of shadows in the early 1950s, although Gardner himself claimed the practice of keeping a book of shadows was ancient. Gardner's book of shadows was composed with the help of Doreen Valiente (1922–1999), a British Wiccan who assisted in bringing Wicca to the attention of the general public through her several books on the subject.

USES

Wiccans believe books of shadows are sacred tools that should only be kept and used by those active in the Wiccan religion. But even if you're not a witch, there is wisdom to be gained from reading books of shadows that are publicly available. Many Wiccans post their books of shadows online, and you can also borrow these books from the library or buy them from various online and brick-and-mortar booksellers.

Channeling

ORIGINS

Channeling is the practice of serving as a medium through which a spirit communicates with a living person. This can take two forms: In the first, the medium serves as the middleman in a conversation between a spirit and a client (often a bereaved relative or spouse). In the second, the medium goes into a trance wherein he or she vacates his or her physical body and allows the spirit to use it to communicate directly with the client. In the latter case, the medium may not be aware of the conversation taking place.

HISTORY/LORE

Attempting to communicate with the dead is an ancient practice found in many cultures. Shamans and witch doctors traditionally contacted the spirits. Channeling gained widespread popularity through the rise of Spiritualism, a nineteenth-century religious movement in the United States and the United Kingdom. Spiritualism is based on the beliefs that the spirits of the dead both desire and are able to communicate with the living, that spirits are more advanced than the living, and that spirits can give the living useful knowledge that they can apply in their lives.

USES

You can try your luck with a Ouija board, but if you're serious about contacting spirits, you should consult an experienced and respected medium. If you hope to contact the spirit of a deceased loved one, it is advised that you let some time pass before visiting a medium. This is to allow your grief to subside a bit (overwhelming expressions of grief could disrupt the medium's process) and also because spirits are not always ready to communicate shortly after death.

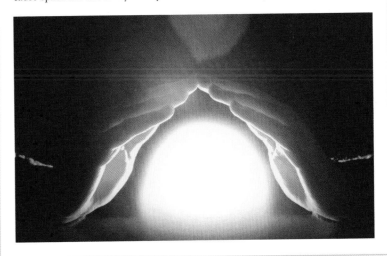

Crystal Ball

ORIGINS

A crystal ball is a globe made of quartz crystal or glass used to see spiritual visions, a practice known as scrying. Sometimes this is done with the purpose of predicting the future, although many believe that the images seen are simply a reflection of one's own subconscious thoughts or imagination.

HISTORY/LORE

The Druids, a priestly caste among the ancient Celtic people who appear as prophets and sorcerers in Welsh and Irish legend, are believed to have been the first to use crystal balls. In the Middle Ages, use of crystal balls by fortune tellers was widespread. John Dee (1527–1608/9) was an adviser to Queen Elizabeth I who devoted much of his life to the study of divination. The British Museum in London holds a crystal ball that supposedly belonged to Dee.

USES

Anyone can buy a crystal ball, and indeed there are many on the market, both in stores and online. Some people use crystal balls in much the same way they use crystals and gemstones—for healing, magical, or spiritual practices (see Chapter 1)—and crystal balls require similar care, such as cleansing and charging. If you're new to crystal balls, though, it is recommended that you visit a professional seer to see what this practice is all about.

Dowsing

ORIGINS

Dowsing is the practice of searching for water, minerals, or other materials underground using a Y-shaped rod called a dowsing or divining rod. The dowser holds one branch of the Y in each hand so that the stem of the Y is pointing straight ahead. Then the dowser

walks slowly over places where he suspects the materials might be found. When the dowsing rod dips toward the ground, it is indicating where the discovery will be made. Alternatively, a pair of L-shaped rods may be used. The dowser holds one rod in each hand (holding the short leg of the L) and walks over the area in the same manner. When the two rods cross each other, X marks the spot.

HISTORY/LORE

Dowsing originated in Germany in the fifteenth century as an attempt to find metals. The German priest and professor Martin Luther (1483–1546), an important figure in the Protestant Reformation, denounced dowsing for metals as an act of occultism that therefore broke the first of the Ten Commandments: "You shall have no other gods before Me." More modern applications of dowsing include searching for buried human remains, locating archaeological sites, and detecting energy fields.

USES

These days, dowsing is not recognized as a scientific way to locate materials underground (in fact, many studies have shown that its probability of success is no greater than pure chance), but that doesn't stop lots of people from dabbling with dowsing as a hobby. If you're interested in trying it yourself, check out some of the many websites and books devoted to the practice. Some claim that a natural sensitivity to certain phenomena, such as Earth's magnetism, is required for successful dowsing, while others say it is a skill like any other that can be developed with practice.

Dream Interpretation

ORIGINS

When our bodies go to sleep at night, our minds remain active, producing dreams—whether we remember them or not. Some dreams are bizarre and otherworldly, and others feel so real that we're surprised (and often relieved) when we wake up. But what, if anything, do dreams mean? Dream interpretation is the practice of assigning meaning to our dreams, which we then apply to our lives in different ways. A dream dictionary is a tool used for interpreting dreams that includes specific images or situations found in dreams, such as a car, a house, a school, falling, or death.

HISTORY/LORE

Humans have always been fascinated by dreams. The ancient Egyptians believed that dreams were a means of divine intervention and had priests interpret their messages. The ancient Greeks took dreams to be omens of things to come. The Austrian neurologist and "father of psychoanalysis," Sigmund Freud (1856–1939), asserted that dreams are a form of wish fulfillment—subconscious attempts to solve conflicts and act out our deepest impulses. In his book *The Interpretation of Dreams*, Freud wrote that the messages in dreams are disguised in order to get them past the "censor" of the preconscious; thus, dreams have to be decoded or interpreted for their true meanings. The Swiss psychotherapist Carl Jung (1875–1961) took Freud's theory one step further and proposed two approaches to interpreting dreams: the objective and the subjective. In the objective approach, the people in a dream represent who they actually are: Your mother is your mother, your father is your father, etc. In the subjective approach, each person in a dream represents some part of yourself: For example, if there is a mother in a dream, that person represents maternal aspects of the dreamer.

USES

Interpreting your dreams can be fun and enlightening. The first step is to record your dreams in detail so that you don't forget them. Keeping a dream journal (see the entry in this chapter) is a great way to do this. Next, you can consult a dream dictionary (there are many available online) or a dream interpreter to discover the meaning behind a given dream. Depending on the resource or person you consult, you may get either a vague or specific interpretation. For example, falling in a dream may represent general fears or anxieties about something in your life, or it may mean that a specific part of your life—your job, your relationship—is rapidly moving in the wrong direction.

Dream Journal

ORIGINS

As discussed in the previous entry on dream interpretation, our dreams may contain important information or messages that we can then apply to our lives. However, this information is of no help to us if we can't recall our dreams, which tend to fade away soon after waking. A dream journal is a great solution to this problem, and getting started is as simple as keeping a notebook and a pen next to your bed. Then you simply record your dreams as soon as you wake up so you can capture them in the greatest detail possible. In addition to recording the content of the dream, you may also choose to record your own interpretation of the dream for future reflection. The act of keeping a dream journal is believed to assist with future dream recall, and it can be particularly helpful in the pursuit of lucid dreams—dreams in which the dreamer is aware that he or she is dreaming.

HISTORY/LORE

The origin of the dream journal is unknown, but it has existed in some form or another for thousands of years. The earliest evidence of recorded dreams was found on 5,000-year-old Mesopotamian clay tablets. The ancient Egyptians recorded their dreams using hieroglyphics and proposed interpretations. The ancient Greeks and Romans also recorded their dreams, believing they were messages from deities or the deceased and that they could predict the future. The Greek philosopher Aristotle (384–322 B.C.E.) wrote about lucid dreams, observing that "often, when one is asleep, there is something in consciousness which declares that what then presents itself is but a dream."

USES

Many people keep a dream journal and perform dream interpretation as a hobby, while others treat it as a more serious component of an intellectual, psychological, or spiritual endeavor or practice. In any case, it's easy to start a dream journal and see where it takes you. If you prefer to keep a digital dream journal instead of a paper one, there are several apps that you can use to record your dreams using your smartphone, tablet, or computer. You might also consider using an audio recording device to narrate and record your dreams orally.

ESP

ORIGINS

ESP, which stands for extrasensory perception, is the ability to receive information using the mind rather than the five physical senses (sight, hearing, smell, taste, and touch). It is also known as the sixth sense. There are many types of ESP, including clairvoyance (paranormal seeing), clairaudience (paranormal hearing), and clairsentience (paranormal sensing or feeling). For example, a clairvoyant individual has the ability to "see" events or people that do not exist in the present time, a clairaudient person is able to "hear" past or future events or voices, and a clairsentient person can "feel" the emotions of others.

HISTORY/LORE

Beginning in the late 1920s, while employed at the newly founded Duke University, the American botanist J.B. Rhine (1895–1980) and his wife, Louisa, performed research in a field they called "parapsychology," which covers such abilities as telepathy, clairvoyance, and precognition. Parapsychology built on the existing field of "psychical" research, whose main goal was to find evidence of an afterlife. In one of the Rhines's ESP experiments, a "sender" would look at a set of ESP cards bearing a series of symbols, and the "receiver" would say which symbol was on each card. The Rhines's work led to the development of the Duke Parapsychology Laboratory in 1935 and the official recognition of parapsychology as a field of experimental science.

USES

Despite the controversial nature of the topic (and flat-out rejection by a significant swath of the scientific community), the field of parapsychology still exists today, although in a much different form than it did when the Rhines created it. Their experiments with cards have been replaced by more modern techniques that measure the physiological characteristics of psychics and healers, among other methods. Some say that we all have psychic abilities that we simply need to uncover and hone, while others believe that only a select few are born with these abilities. Whatever your stance on the issue, there is a seemingly endless array of books, films, websites, and other media that deal with the topic of ESP, allowing anyone to make a hobby out of studying (and even practicing) this fascinating phenomenon.

Graphology

ORIGINS

Graphology is the analysis of handwriting for the purpose of discovering something about the writer. Graphology has many applications, from employment procedures to criminal psychology, but in the New Age sense, it is simply an interesting way to learn about one's personality and character traits. There are numerous systems of handwriting analysis, including integrative, which looks at how strokes are used; symbolic, which looks for symbols in the handwriting; and holistic, which looks at the handwriting as a whole.

HISTORY/LORE

The Italian philosopher Camillo Baldi (1550–1637) published what is generally recognized as the first book on graphology in 1622. The French priest and archaeologist Jean-Hippolyte Michon (1806–1881), who wrote and lectured widely on the topic of handwriting analysis, is said to have coined the term *graphology*. Graphotherapy, the practice of changing a person's handwriting with the goal of changing his or her personality, originated in France in the 1930s and later spread to the United States.

USES

As a non-professional pursuit, handwriting analysis is a fun way to learn more about yourself and others. An easy way to get started is to read up on the topic and perhaps take a graphology test (there are many available online). You could also take some graphology classes, such as those offered through the American Society of Professional Graphologists (ASPG). The ASPG website (*www.aspg handwriting.org*) has some interesting resources, including analyzed samples of famous people's handwriting.

I Ching

ORIGINS

The I Ching, or the Book of Changes, is an ancient Chinese text containing sixty-four interrelated hexagrams originally used for divination, along with commentaries attributed to the Chinese philosopher Confucius (551–479 B.C.E.). The hexagrams represent nature and human endeavor in terms of yin and yang—the seemingly opposing and yet complementary forces of the natural world. The I Ching uses a type of divination called cleromancy, in which an outcome is determined by seemingly random means (such as flipping a coin or rolling a die) but was once believed to reveal the will of God.

HISTORY/LORE

The I Ching has evolved over the course of thousands of years. The text originated in a Western Zhou divination book called the *Zhou yi*, which was assembled between the tenth and the fourth centuries B.C.E. The *Zhou yi* offered a guide to cleromancy using the stalks of the yarrow plant (see entry in Chapter 2), although it is not clear how the stalks translated to the numbers or lines used in the hexagrams. Ultimately, the I Ching evolved into the cosmological text we know today with a series of commentaries known as the "Ten Wings."

USES

If you're new to the I Ching, you may be a bit overwhelmed by its ancient origins and apparent complexity. Hexagrams? Yarrow stalks? How is a person supposed to use this thing anyway? Worry not; there are many modern interpretations and techniques that simplify the act of consulting the I Ching for guidance and wisdom, one of which is a series of coin tosses you can perform. There are lots of online resources with step-by-step instructions for using the I Ching, as well as countless books, classes, and workshops for those interested in this ancient text and its modern applications.

Numerology

ORIGINS

Numerology is the study of numbers, their meanings, and their effects on human life. There are many different forms of numerology that originated in cultures all over the world. Gematria, for instance is a system that assigns numerical value to a word or phrase. An example is the Hebrew word *Chai*, meaning "alive," which translates to the number 18, making this a lucky number among the Jewish people. Birthdates are considered important numbers in numerology, and the "life path" number is the sum of a person's birth date.

HISTORY/LORE

Numerology has its roots in ancient Greece and the studies of philosophers and mathematicians such as Pythagoras (c. 570–c. 495 B.C.E.) who believed numbers were the universal language of truth. In the Arabic system of numerology, each letter of the Arabic alphabet has a numerical value. In Chinese numerology, even numbers are considered lucky, due to the belief that good luck comes in pairs.

USES

There is no limit to how deep you can go into the practice of numerology. A quick online search will reveal countless resources about this ancient system. But if you're new to numerology, you probably want to start with the basics. Try one of the many websites that will generate your numerology chart based on the letters of your name and your birth date. You can also calculate your own life path number by adding up the digits of your birth date. For example, if you were born on October 23, 1972, the equation is $10 + 23 + 1972 = 2005$. Then you add those digits together: $2 + 0 + 0 + 5 = 7$. Once you know your life path number, you can learn about the meanings behind this number. Another fun way to explore numerology is to have your numbers read by a professional numerologist.

Palmistry

ORIGINS

Palmistry, also called palm reading or hand analysis, is the practice of foretelling the future based on the lines, marks, and patterns on the palms of the hands. There are two main approaches to this practice: Chiromancy deals with the lines on the palm, and chirognomy deals with the shape of the hands and the color, shape, and texture of the palm and fingers.

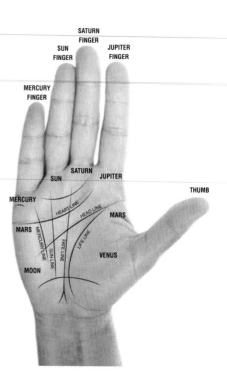

HISTORY/LORE

Palmistry is an ancient practice. While the exact timing is unknown, historians believe it originated in India and then spread to China, Egypt, Greece, and eventually Europe. The Greek philosopher Aristotle (384–322 B.C.E.) observed, "Lines are not written into the human hand without reason. They emanate from heavenly influences and man's own individuality." During the Middle Ages, the Catholic Church condemned the practice of palmistry, declaring it a pagan superstition. One of the major figures of palmistry's revival in the nineteenth century was Captain Casimir Stanislas D'Arpentigny (1798–1872), a Frenchman who is credited as the first person to formulate a system of hand-shape classification. In his 1938 book, *How to Know People by Their Hands*, palmist Josef Ranald analyzed the handprints of Franklin Delano Roosevelt, Benito Mussolini, and Adolf Hitler.

USES

Despite its historical ups and downs, today the practice of palmistry is alive and well. If you're interested in having your palm read, just search for a reputable palm reader in your area (chances are, there will be more than one). If, on the other hand (no pun intended), you're interested in learning the art of palm reading yourself, there are countless resources out there, from books to websites and beyond. Organizations such as the American Professional Palmistry Association (*www.palmistrylessons.com*) and the International Institute of Hand Analysis (*www.handanalysis.net*) offer classes, materials, and online resources.

Past-Life Recall

ORIGINS

In various cultures, it is believed that the lives we are currently living are not our first—or our last. Hindus and Buddhists, for example, believe in reincarnation, the rebirth of the soul (or spirit or consciousness) in another body after death. Many who believe in reincarnation also believe that it is possible to recall our past lives through various practices such as hypnosis and meditation. Past-life recall is the process of remembering those former lives and gleaning information from them that can assist us in the present.

HISTORY/LORE

The Upanishads, a collection of ancient Vedic Sanskrit texts that contributed to the theology of ancient Hinduism, mention both reincarnation and past-life recall, specifically past-life regression, a form of past-life recall using hypnosis. The French psychologist and philosopher (and contemporary of Freud) Pierre Janet (1859–1947) is recognized as one of the first people to make a connection between the events in a subject's past life and his or her present-day trauma. Both Janet and Freud experimented with past-life regression as a therapeutic tool.

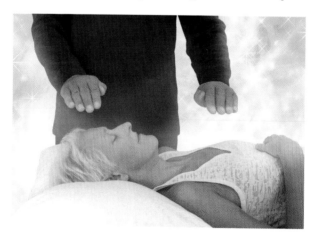

USES

In a *New York Times* article from 2010, Cornell-trained psychiatrist Dr. Paul DeBell stated that belief in reincarnation "allows you to experience history as yours. It gives you a different sense of what it means to be human." If this interests you, then past-life recall is for you. You can explore the practice on your own or with the assistance of a hypnotist, therapist, or other specialist. There are countless books, websites, and other resources that offer information on past-life recall for beginners, including specialists who are practicing in your area. As discussed in Chapter 1, amber and opal are two stones that can be used in meditation to help remember past lives. Burning rosemary during meditation or dream work also aids in past-life recall (see Chapter 2).

Pendulum

ORIGINS

A pendulum is an item that swings freely from a fixed point under the influence of gravity. You are probably familiar with pendulums as the timekeeping elements of certain types of clocks, but they have many other applications. They are used in religious traditions as well as practices such as dowsing (see entry in this chapter). Pendulums also have a variety of spiritual and healing uses.

HISTORY/LORE

The Italian astronomer, physicist, engineer, philosopher, and mathematician Galileo Galilei (1564–1642) became interested in the study of pendulums after observing a swinging chandelier. He went on to make an important discovery about pendulums: The time it takes for a pendulum to complete one swing remains almost exactly the same, regardless of the size of the arc it makes. Building on Galilei's work, the Dutch scientist Christiaan Huygens (1629–1695) built the first pendulum clock in 1656. Censers—incense burners that swing at the end of a chain—appear in various religious and cultural traditions, such as Catholicism.

USES

Radiesthesia is the use of a pendulum to locate an object or substance or to assess the energy (or "radiation") of a subject. One example of this is dowsing, which was discussed earlier in this chapter. Instead of using a dowsing rod to locate water or minerals underground, a pendulum may be used. The process is very similar: You assign meanings to the various movements of the pendulum (for example, swinging from left to right means there is water) and then walk slowly over the search area. Another way to use pendulums is to get answers to questions about your life. You simply "program" the pendulum (deciding which movement means "yes" and which means "no"), and then you ask questions out loud and wait for answers. Pendulums are also used for locating imbalances in the chakras and detecting illness.

Runes

ORIGINS

Runes are the letters of a set of related alphabets used by ancient Germanic peoples prior to the adoption of the Latin alphabet. However, runes were much more than letters as we think of them today; each rune was a symbol of a principle or power, and it was believed that writing a rune invoked the force it represented. In addition to general writing purposes, runes were used to make calendars, encode secret messages, and cast spells. The word *rune* comes from the Old English *run*, meaning "whisper, talk in secret."

HISTORY/LORE

Runes are believed to have derived from one of the many Old Italic alphabets used by the Mediterranean peoples of the first century C.E. The runic alphabets were in use between the third and the thirteenth centuries and were replaced with Latin through the process of Christianization in Europe. The Meldorf brooch (also called the Meldorf fibula) bears what is possibly the oldest known runic inscription. It was discovered in Meldorf, Schleswig-Holstein, Germany, in 1979 and dates back to the mid–first century C.E. However, scholars disagree on whether this inscription is truly runic or proto-runic.

USES

Like the I Ching or tarot (see entries in this chapter), you can use runes to receive messages and spiritual insight. You can visit a rune reader for an experience that is somewhat similar to a tarot card reading, or you can learn how to cast runes and read them yourself. Begin by reading up on runes and buying a set of your own. They are usually in the form of small tiles or pebbles and may be made of wood, stone, crystal, metal, or even bone. Rune reading is not to be confused with fortune telling; the runes don't give you direct advice or exact answers. Instead, they offer hints and variables and leave you to work out the details using your intuition.

Scrying Mirror

ORIGINS

Scrying is the practice of gleaning information from images "seen" in a reflective, translucent, or luminescent surface. But this is not like looking at your own reflection in the bathroom mirror; instead, the images seen reflect inner spiritual visions. A scrying mirror may be made of a variety of materials, such as crystals, glass, or water. The word *scry* is actually short for *descry*, which means to catch sight of or detect. *Descry* comes from the Old French *descrier*, meaning "to call, cry out." (See also the crystal ball entry in this chapter.)

HISTORY/LORE

Today, the visions received through scrying are thought to come from one's own subconscious, imagination, or inner spirit, while in the past it was believed they came from gods, spirits, or other divine or ethereal influences. The legendary Cup of Jamshid is a famous scrying mirror that appears in Persian mythology. The cup was said to be filled with an elixir of immortality in which the whole world was reflected. The French apothecary and seer Nostradamus (1503–1566) used a bowl of clear water for scrying and then wrote about his visions. Joseph Smith Jr. (1805–1844) founded the Mormon religion based in part on information obtained through the reflections in seer stones.

USES

Although some firmly believe that only a select few possess scrying abilities, the general consensus is that anyone can learn this ancient art with practice. To begin, get yourself a scrying mirror. You can purchase one in a store or on-line, or you can make one yourself. There is a wide variety of options out there in terms of materials and forms. As you learned in Chapter 1, malachite, obsidian, and tourmaline are stones that can be used for scrying. You could also try Nostradamus's bowl-of-water technique. Next, you must achieve a meditative or trance-like state that allows for deep inner focus and exploration. Finally, with practice, visions will appear. There are countless resources, including books, websites, and organizations, where you can learn specific scrying methods and how to interpret the visions you see.

Shamanic Journeying

ORIGINS

A shaman is a person who acts as a medium between the visible physical world (ordinary reality) and the invisible spirit world (non-ordinary reality). Shamans have different roles depending on the culture, but in general they perform healing, divination, and other rituals and practices. A shamanic journey is a process in which a shaman enters an altered state of consciousness and then travels to the spirit world for any number of reasons—to heal the sick, locate lost souls, or glean information about the future.

HISTORY/LORE

Shamanism is an ancient spiritual practice dating back tens of thousands of years. It has existed in many cultures worldwide, from the Mayan and Aztec people of Mexico and Central and South America to the Hmong people of China. The American anthropologist, educator, and author Michael Harner (born 1929) is a major figure in contemporary Western shamanism. He founded the Foundation for Shamanic Studies and wrote the classic book *The Way of the Shaman.*

USES

In some cultural traditions, a person must be "called" or born into shamanism, or at least undergo extensive training. Others believe that anyone can attempt to contact the spirits while in an altered state of consciousness. If you're interested in trying shamanic journeying, there are many methods available. One is to listen to a repetitive sound, such as drumming or rattling, to achieve a meditative, trance-like state. Once this state is achieved, your journey may take any number of forms. It may feel like meditation—a deep exploration of your inner self—or you may have the opportunity to communicate with spirits, who could appear to be people or animals (see the spirit animal appearances entry in this chapter). For assistance with your method and interpreting what you see on your journey, consult some of the many resources available in print or online (such as the Foundation for Shamanic Studies website, *www.shamanism.org*), or seek the guidance of a shaman, healer, or other specialist.

Spirit Animal Appearances

ORIGINS

Spirit animals (also known as spirit guides or power animals) are spirits that appear as animals in dreams or visions achieved through various spiritual practices, such as meditation and shamanic journeying (see entry in this chapter). Each animal has its own significance or meaning, but these meanings vary widely depending on which tradition you consult. Spirit animals are similar to totems found in some indigenous cultures.

HISTORY/LORE

The concept of spirit animals originated in ancient totemistic and animistic traditions. Totemism, a system practiced by the Native Americans and the Australian Aborigines, among others, includes the belief that every human being has a spiritual connection to another living being, such as a particular animal. Animism is related belief held by Neopagans and other groups that non-human entities (including animals, plants, and in some cases even inanimate objects) have individual spirits. The ancient Greek philosopher Pythagoras (c. 570–c. 495 B.C.E.) is quoted as saying, "Animals share with us the privilege of having a soul." Michael Harner's book *The Way of the Shaman* includes a chapter on power animals.

USES

It is generally believed that you do not choose your spirit animal; it chooses you. You may see the same animal over and over in dreams, or you may have repeated encounters with a certain animal in your waking life. In scrying practices, visions may include animals, and in meditation and shamanic journeying, animal spirit guides may appear and offer guidance. Once you have discovered your spirit animal, your task is to learn its significance and discern any messages it is trying to relay to you. There are numerous spirit animal guides available online, and you can also seek the guidance of a healer, shaman, or other specialist to learn the meaning and messages of your spirit animal.

Tarot

ORIGINS

The tarot is a deck of usually seventy-eight cards that were originally created for card games but now are also used for divination. The deck is divided into two sections: the major arcana (twenty-two cards) and the minor arcana (fifty-six cards). Each card features a specific concept or archetype—for example, Justice or The Lovers. It is believed that the cards you select can provide answers to questions and show you what you need to see in order to make certain decisions and moves in life.

HISTORY/LORE

The tarot (originally known as *trionfi*) originated in the mid-fifteenth century in Europe, where it is still used to play card games. It wasn't until the eighteenth century that tarot card reading first appeared as a divination practice. The French occultist Jean-Baptiste Alliette (1738–1791), also known by the pseudonym Etteilla, is credited with popularizing tarot as a divination method and issuing the first tarot deck created specifically for this purpose.

USES

There are two ways to get involved with the tarot: You can visit a tarot card reader and have your cards read, or you can learn the art of tarot card reading yourself—or both! Many people have their cards read only when they feel they need guidance or want to reflect on where they are in life, while others do it on a regular basis. Tarot card readings are relatively quick (as short as fifteen minutes) and typically very affordable, so it's worth trying if you've never had the experience. Once you've had your first reading, you may feel inspired to buy your own deck and learn how to read the cards yourself. There are endless resources that can help you do this, including online courses, workshops, books, and websites.

Vision Quest

ORIGINS

A vision quest is a Native American rite of passage that has been adapted as a New Age practice. Traditionally, you spend time alone in a natural environment with the objective of forging a connection with yourself and the forces of nature. During this period of seclusion, you may receive insight in the form of a vision that relates to your purpose in life. Depending on the tradition, a vision quest may also involve fasting and/or altering your state of consciousness.

HISTORY/LORE

Vision quests are performed in many Native American cultures, and each has its own nuances and specifications. In traditional Lakota culture, for example, young teenagers undergo a vision quest known as Hembleciya, which means "crying for a vision or dream." Before beginning the quest, the quester spends time in a sweat lodge to cleanse the mind and body. Then, a medicine man prepares the quester by offering information, guidance, and sometimes a substance to help alter the person's consciousness. When the quester returns, he or she discusses the experience with the medicine man, who offers interpretations and advice for how to proceed.

USES

Anyone can undertake a vision quest, but there is potential for serious danger if you are not adequately prepared. To ensure a successful experience, seek the counsel of a vision quest expert before setting out, or try a guided vision quest instead of going solo. If you are going to be fasting, altering your state of consciousness, or questing in a location where the elements could cause you problems, make sure you have safety precautions in place and alert loved ones to your plans before beginning your quest.

8

The Power of Symbols

Symbols appear in almost every area of our lives. From the colors that brighten our world to the numbers and words we use to quantify and communicate, human society functions largely through the use of symbols. The word *symbol* comes from the Greek *sumbolon*, meaning "token for identification."

The subjects in this chapter play important roles in many of the other topics discussed in this book. While reading about the power of stones in Chapter 1, you learned how their color is used in the ancient Chinese practice of feng shui, as well as how it relates to the chakras, or energy centers, of our bodies. You also discovered how numbers are used in studies such as the I Ching and numerology (see entries in Chapter 7). In addition to colors and numbers, in this chapter we'll discuss the importance of shapes, sigils, and words as symbols throughout history and in our modern-day lives.

Colors

ORIGINS

What we identify as color is really just the perception by our eyes and brains of the spectrum of light and its interaction with objects and materials. The perception of color also varies by individual and by species. Those who are colorblind lack the ability to see certain colors or to distinguish between colors. Dogs and cats see in color, but they can't see all the colors that their human companions do. As a symbol, color plays a central role in almost everything we do, from singing the blues to stopping at red lights.

HISTORY/LORE

Humans have always used color as a form of expression, the earliest evidence of which is cave paintings from the Paleolithic era. The ancient Egyptians used color to represent specific characteristics. For instance, Osiris, the god of the afterlife, the underworld, and the dead, is always depicted with green skin—the color of rebirth. Many of the ancient Greek and Roman statues carved in white marble that survived to the present day—such as the Lovatelli Venus from the first century C.E.—once bore bright paint colors that wore off over time. Color also plays an important role in religion. In Christianity, for example, purple is associated with penance and is used during the seasons of Advent and Lent.

USES

There are many fields that feature color symbolism. Color psychology, for instance, is the study of how color affects human behavior. Professionals in this field have made fascinating discoveries and even instituted changes based on color that have improved our daily lives. For example, based on evidence that the color blue has a calming effect, in 2000, the city of Glasgow, Scotland, instituted blue streetlights in certain areas and found that crime decreased as a result.

Numbers

ORIGINS

As discussed in the numerology entry in Chapter 7, numbers can be used for much more than arithmetic. They have many New Age applications, from divination to healing. One concept in the study of numbers that relates to the New Age realm is infinity—space, time, or a quantity with no limit—which is prominent in the areas of both theology and philosophy. As symbols, numbers hold great importance in various religious, cultural, and other traditions.

HISTORY/LORE

Tallying is considered the first abstract numerical system. Place value systems came next, such as the Mesopotamian base 60 system (c. 3400 B.C.E.) and the Egyptian base 10 system (c. 3100 B.C.E.). One of the most important historical figures in relation to numbers is the ancient Greek philosopher and mathematician Pythagoras (c. 570–c. 495 B.C.E.), who believed that numbers were the basis of the entire universe. A school of philosophy based on his beliefs called Pythagoreanism emerged in the fifth century B.C.E. Certain numbers have special significance in different cultures. For example, while the ancient Egyptians considered thirteen a lucky number, in the modern-day Western world, this number is considered so unlucky that there is a phobia associated with it (triskaidekaphobia).

USES

As previously mentioned, numerology is one popular New Age use of numbers (see the numerology entry in Chapter 7). Another is using numbers in magical practices. There are many spells and rituals that incorporate numbers, based on the belief that each number has its own magic properties. You might choose to use a certain number of candles in a spell, or begin a ritual on a certain day of the month. Birth numbers and personal lucky numbers are especially good for this.

Shapes

ORIGINS

Shapes are fundamental to the way we see and interpret the world around us. From simple geometric shapes such as the circle and the square to more elaborate shapes like the triskelion—an ancient symbol consisting of three bent or curved lines radiating from a common center—shapes carry

profound meanings in various religious and cultural traditions as well as New Age practices. The word *shape* comes from the Old English *gesceap*, meaning "a creation."

HISTORY/LORE

The origins of geometry, the branch of mathematics concerned with the shape, size, and relative position of figures, can be traced to ancient Mesopotamia and Egypt around 2000 B.C.E. The ancient Greek mathematician Euclid (birth and death dates unknown, though he was known to be active around 300 B.C.E.) is considered the "father of geometry." Platonic solids are three-dimensional polyhedra named for the ancient Greek philosopher and mathematician Plato (c. 428–348 B.C.E.), who theorized that the "classical elements," an early term for the states of matter, were made of these solids.

USES

One modern-day application for the study of shapes is in the field of psychology. The bouba/kiki effect, which was first observed by the German psychologist Wolfgang Köhler (1887–1967) in the 1920s, suggests that the human brain attaches abstract meanings to shapes and sounds in a consistent way. In his experiment, Köhler showed participants two shapes, one jagged and one rounded, and asked them to identify which was called "takete" and which was called "baluba." The result was a strong preference to call the jagged shape "takete" and the rounded shape "baluba." This experiment was repeated in 2001 using the words "bouba" and "kiki" with the same result: The vast majority of participants paired the rounded shape with "bouba" and the jagged shape with "kiki."

Sigils

ORIGINS

The basic definition of a sigil is a seal, such as one used with melted wax to seal an envelope. However, in the New Age sense, and particularly with regard to magic, a sigil is an image that acts as a symbolic representation of the user's desire or the intended outcome of a magical spell or ritual. The word *sigil* comes from the Latin *signum*, meaning "sign."

HISTORY/LORE

In medieval ceremonial magic, the term *sigil* referred to occult signs representing angels and demons that could be summoned through the practice of magic. These sigils were considered equivalent to the names of these beings and therefore gave the magician a certain amount of control over them. One method of creating these sigils was to convert the names of the angels and demons to numbers, which were then incorporated into "magic squares" (arrangements of numbers in square grids where each number is used only once and each row, column, and diagonal adds up to the same number). When lines were drawn between the numbers, an abstract figure appeared.

USES

Although sigils are typically used by experienced practitioners of magic, any-one can create a sigil and use it in a ritual with the goal of manifesting a desire. Here's a simple process you can follow.

1. Write a simple sentence in all capital letters using the present tense that embodies your desire as if it were already a fact. For example, instead of writing, "I WANT TO BE HAPPY," write, "I AM HAPPY."

2. Cross out any duplicate letters and rewrite the letters that remain: "I A M H P Y."

3. Choose how you will incorporate these letters into a symbol. Some easy options are to use the letters themselves to create an image, or to convert them to numbers or Roman numerals based on their positions in the alphabet. For example, "I" is 9 or IX, "A" is 1 or I, and so on.

4. Once you have created your sigil, you can incorporate it into the ritual or practice of your choice, such as meditation.

Words

ORIGINS

Words are the smallest meaningful units of language that can stand on their own. We use words in both written and spoken form to express ourselves, to communicate with one another, and to document our experiences. Unlike some of the other topics in this chapter, words are purely symbols; their entire purpose is to represent something else—an idea, an object, an emotion, a sound. In the New Age realm, words have various applications, in magic, healing, and other areas.

HISTORY/LORE

Etymology is the branch of linguistics that deals with the history of words, their origins, and how their forms and meanings have changed over time. The word *etymology* comes from the Greek *etumologia*: *etumon*, meaning "true sense of a word," plus *logia*, from *logos*, meaning "one who deals with." It is believed that written language began around 3200 B.C.E. in Mesopotamia.

USES

Words are central to many New Age healing and spiritual practices. Chanting and mantra, covered in Chapter 6, are two examples of ways you can harness the power of words. Another practice, called "imprinting water," combines words and water to create a homeopathic remedy for dealing with emotional issues, energy blockages, or trauma. The idea behind this practice is that words have their own vibrations and water can be imprinted with these vibrations. One way to do this is to write a word, such as *love*, on a piece of paper, tape it to the outside of a glass bottle, and then fill the bottle with water. It is then your choice how you use the water: for drinking, for watering plants, for cooking, etc. It is believed that the energy from the word (and your intention in choosing that word) will then be incorporated in the water's use.

9

The Power of Movement

Lest you think this book is all about sitting still and quietly meditating, in this chapter we're going to talk about an important aspect of the New Age lifestyle: movement! Humans are active beings. We run, jump, swim, stretch, dance, play, and perform, all using our unique, amazing bodies. Not only is movement crucial for our physical health; it's also essential for our mental and emotional well-being. These days it's more important than ever to take some time each day to put down our phones, step away from our computers, and get moving.

The topics covered in this chapter include all types of movement, from the subtle but vital act of breathing to the intricate gestures and postures found in practices like Qi Gong and yoga. Some of these, such as dance, may already be very familiar to you, while others, like mudras, may be mysteries. All the more reason to dive in and learn more about the power of movement, and who knows, by the end of the chapter you may find yourself with a new hobby.

Active Meditation

ORIGINS

Meditation is discussed throughout this book as a spiritual practice that involves sitting or standing quietly and focusing your attention inward to achieve a state of calm or to perform deep personal exploration. However, that's not the only form meditation can take. Active meditation is a style of meditation that includes physical movements, such as jumping or dancing, followed by silence. The movements allow for both physical and emotional release, while giving the mind a break from thought and worry.

HISTORY/LORE

The Indian mystic, guru, and spiritual teacher Osho (1931–1990) created a number of active meditation techniques, which he believed were more applicable to modern life than traditional meditation practices. One such technique is called "dynamic meditation," which involves four stages of movement with music and one stage of silent reflection. Osho's other active meditation methods include kundalini "shaking" meditation, which involves shaking the body and dancing, and nadabrahma "humming" meditation, which involves humming and hand movements. Osho also believed these active meditation techniques served as helpful preparation for more traditional meditation.

USES

Active meditation has many of the same benefits as standard meditation, plus a few bonus perks. In addition to calming the mind, you also get to invigorate the body by using your muscles, getting your heart rate up, and boosting blood circulation. You can practice active meditation alone or in a group setting. There are many online tutorials and videos that can help you practice at home, or you can attend a class, workshop, or retreat in your area. There is also a wide variety of active meditation music available for download or streaming online. As with any type of meditation, it's helpful to set an intention for your session before you begin. You can focus on this intention mentally or announce it out loud as a chant or a mantra (see entries in Chapter 6).

Breathwork

ORIGINS

The breath is central to many New Age practices, including Qi Gong, tai chi, and yoga (see entries in this chapter). But breathwork is also a practice in itself. Consciously controlling our breathing is thought to influence our mental, emotional, and physical states, reducing stress and tension and increasing relaxation and focus. Specific techniques include *pranayama*, Holotropic Breathwork, and integrative breathwork.

HISTORY/LORE

Breathwork is an ancient practice that is integral to countless spiritual and healing endeavors. In Hinduism, the breath is considered the source of the life force (*prana*). *Pranayama* (extension of the life force or breath) is a type of breath control that is incorporated into many spiritual practices. The Czech psychiatrist Stanislav Grof (born 1931) developed Holotropic Breathwork, a trademarked method of accessing "non-ordinary" states of consciousness. Integrative breathwork, described as "an evocative musical journey utilizing breath," was developed by Jacquelyn Small, who founded the Eupsychia Institute in Austin, Texas.

USES

Breathing is a natural, involuntary process. Our bodies do it whether we're thinking about it or not. But taking the time to focus on the breath can have numerous benefits for both the mind and body. When we're not concentrating on it, we often revert to shallow breathing, which means we don't take in as much oxygen as we could. Consciously taking deeper, fuller breaths can help oxygenate the blood, which in turn helps our bodies work better, from our brains to our feet. There are countless ways to use breathwork, from incorporating it into your meditation or yoga routine to practicing it at your desk at work. There are many wonderful breathwork resources available online, but classes and workshops are especially good opportunities to learn from trained breathwork therapists and healers. There are also professional breathwork training programs for those who are interested in becoming practitioners themselves.

Dance

ORIGINS

Dance is one of our most beautiful and satisfying modes of expression. From ballet to hip hop, there is a type of dance for every mood or occasion. In the New Age realm, dance appears in a variety of practices, usually as a form of tension release or physical expression; an example of this is active meditation (see entry in this chapter). Typically, music and dance go hand in hand, as discussed in Chapter 6: The Power of Sound.

HISTORY/LORE

It is likely that humans have been dancing since our very beginning, but the earliest known documentation of dance is found in 9,000-year-old cave paintings discovered at the Bhimbetka rock shelters in Madhya Pradesh, India. Chinese pottery from the Neolithic period features images of people dancing in lines holding hands. In the ancient Egyptian, Greek, and Roman civilizations, dance was a part of life and was incorporated into many ceremonies and rituals, including funerals.

USES

The options are limitless when it comes to dance. Dancing by yourself in the privacy of your own home is a great way to blow off steam and have a little fun, but group classes and workshops offer an opportunity to learn from experienced teachers and to try dances that involve partners or larger groups of people. Many gyms, meditation centers, yoga studios, and other places where you may already have a membership also offer dance classes. Dance/movement therapy is another option you might be interested in checking out. The American Dance Therapy Association defines dance/movement therapy as "the psychotherapeutic use of movement to further the emotional, cognitive, physical and social integration of the individual." Their website (*www.adta.org*) has lots of helpful resources and information.

Labyrinth Walking

ORIGINS

A labyrinth, also known as a maze, is an intricate structure of interconnected passageways through which it's difficult to find your way. Labyrinths have had many purposes throughout history, from deterring or trapping an enemy to enhancing prayer or devotion. Today, many people enjoy the New Age practice of labyrinth walking, which consists of walking through the passages of a labyrinth as part of spiritual exploration, contemplation, or prayer. The experience simulates the path of life, which is full of twists and turns and where the future is always just out of view.

HISTORY/LORE

In Greek mythology, King Minos of Crete commanded the architect and artist Daedalus to design and build a labyrinth to hold the Minotaur, a creature with the head of a bull and the body of a man. The Minotaur was eventually killed by the hero Theseus. As the story goes, the labyrinth was so complex that even its creator had trouble escaping from it.

Labyrinths also appear in the Christian tradition. An example is the labyrinth in the Chartres Cathedral in France, which was constructed in the early thirteenth century. Though little documentation exists, it is believed that labyrinths such as the one in Chartres symbolize the long, arduous path that pilgrims would have followed to visit places of worship during the medieval period.

USES

This is one of the few practices in this book that you can't undertake on your own—assuming you don't have a labyrinth in your backyard or the space to build one. Luckily, there are labyrinths all over the world that are open to the public. The website *www.labyrinthos.net* has a "worldwide labyrinth locator" as well as a photo library and various other resources. Another great resource is the nonprofit organization Veriditas (*www.veriditas.org*), whose mission is to inspire "personal and planetary change and renewal through the labyrinth experience."

Mudras

ORIGINS

Mudras are symbolic gestures and movements that are featured in Hinduism and Buddhism, and also appear in classical Indian dance, meditation, yoga, and tantric practice. Although some mudras involve the entire body, most are performed with the hands. In yoga, mudras are often used in combination with *pranayama* breathwork (see the breathwork entry in this chapter). The word *mudra* comes from the Sanskrit *mudra*, meaning "seal, mystery."

HISTORY/LORE

During the Vedic period in India (c. 1750–500 B.C.E.), mudras were performed during the chanting of the Vedas, the ancient scriptural texts of Hinduism. When Buddhism emerged in the sixth century B.C.E., the use of mudras was expanded to Buddhist rituals, iconography, and meditation practices. In Indian classical dance, mudras involve hand, arm, and body movements as well as facial expressions. Various Asian martial arts also make use of mudras.

USES

In addition to being interesting and fun, mudras can take your spiritual practice to the next level. By performing these gestures and movements, you can enhance the flow of energy, which can benefit the mind, body, and spirit. One well-known mudra you may already be familiar with is the chin mudra, which is commonly used during seated meditation. While sitting cross-legged or in lotus position, place the hands on the knees palm up and join the tip of the index finger and thumb of each hand. The circle created by the fingers signifies unity and facilitates the flow of energy. There are hundreds of other mudras you can learn about online or by taking classes or workshops in practices such as kundalini yoga (see the yoga entry in this chapter).

Qi Gong

ORIGINS

Qi Gong is a Chinese spiritual practice in which physical exercises or movements are performed in a meditative state with the purpose of aligning the body, breath, and mind and cultivating and balancing qi (chi), or "life energy." Qi Gong is a part of many healing and spiritual practices as well as martial arts training techniques. The term *Qi Gong* comes from the Mandarin *qigong*: *qi*, meaning "air, spirit, energy of life," plus *gong*, meaning "skill."

HISTORY/LORE

Qi Gong is estimated to be more than 4,000 years old, with roots in ancient shamanic rituals consisting of meditative practice and gymnastic exercise. Over time, Qi Gong was adopted into other practices and traditions, such as Chinese medicine, Confucianism, Taoism, and Buddhism. Two important figures in modern Qi Gong are Jiang Weiqiao (1873–1958), who was one of the first Qi Gong experts to introduce the exercises to the public, and Liu Guizhen (1920–1983), who is credited with coining the term *Qi Gong*.

USES

Qi Gong is not only an enlightening spiritual practice; it also has numerous health benefits, from stress relief to increasing flexibility and strength. The best way to get started is to attend a class or workshop so you can receive in-person instruction and guidance from an experienced teacher. If there are no offerings in your area, don't worry; the Internet has plenty of Qi Gong information and tutorials. The National Qigong Association hosts an annual Qi Gong conference, and their website (*http://nqa.org*) is a terrific source of information about the practice as well as upcoming events across the country.

Ritual Movements

ORIGINS

Ritual movements are any movements or gestures that are performed as part of a ritual or ceremony, such as bowing one's head or pressing one's hands together during prayer. These movements may express a person's intention in performing the ritual, such as atonement, or they may serve as preparation, such as striking a certain pose or preparing the body in some way. The word *ritual* comes from the Latin *ritus*, meaning "rite."

HISTORY/LORE

Ritual movements are a component of many ancient religious and spiritual practices. A common ritual movement performed in Catholicism is making the sign of the cross with one's hand. The fingertips first touch the forehead, then the lower middle of the chest, then the left shoulder, and finally the right shoulder. In Islam, a series of movements accompanies daily prayers, which are performed five times a day at specific times. These movements include kneeling on a prayer rug, facing the direction of Mecca, the birthplace of the prophet Muhammad. The worshiper bends down to place his head and hands on the floor.

USES

Ritual movements are included in most religious practices, usually in combination with prayer. If you were raised with or currently practice a religion, chances are you are familiar with several ritual movements already. If not, you may have learned ritual movements through practices such as meditation or performing magic. For example, incense is often used in combination with movements to waft the smoke toward oneself or throughout a space in preparation for meditation or to cleanse a space of negative influences. Whatever ritual movements you choose to try, you will probably find that they add another dimension to your practice, and over time you may feel that they have become a necessary part of your ritual or routine.

Tai Chi

ORIGINS

Tai chi is a Chinese martial art that is closely related to Qi Gong (see entry in this chapter) and practiced in various styles, from fast-paced self-defense techniques to slow-paced meditative movements. The term *tai chi* comes from the Mandarin *tài jí quán*: *tài jí*, meaning "great, ultimate," and *quán*, meaning "boxing."

HISTORY/LORE

The origins of tai chi are largely unknown. One legend says that a Taoist monk named Chang San-Feng created tai chi based on the movements of animals. (In fact, some of the movements are named for animals and various natural phenomena—for example, "embrace tiger, return to mountain.") It is more likely, though, that tai chi is rooted in a combination of Chinese philosophy (such as the concepts of chi and yin/yang) and martial arts such as kung fu. Today, the practice of tai chi continues in China and beyond. World Tai Chi and Qigong Day (*www.worldtaichiday.org*) is celebrated on the last Saturday of April each year in hundreds of cities across the globe.

USES

The three main reasons to practice tai chi are health, meditation, and self-defense. Tai chi is an excellent stress reliever that has been shown to ease anxiety and depression, lower blood pressure, and improve the quality of sleep. As a meditative practice, it serves to keep you grounded in your body and in the present moment. And while the slower styles of tai chi may not seem very helpful in the realm of self-defense, the movements are the foundations of powerful, fast, and effective martial arts techniques.

Yoga

ORIGINS

Yoga is an ancient Indian physical, mental, and spiritual practice that incorporates controlled breathing, prescribed body postures, and meditation. While it is not always practiced as part of a religion, yoga is an integral component of the Hindu and Buddhist traditions. There are numerous styles of yoga, including hatha, kundalini, and ashtanga. The word *yoga* comes from the Sanskrit *yogah*, meaning "union, joining."

HISTORY/LORE

As a result of the oral transmission and once-secretive nature of yoga's history, it is not known exactly when the practice began. It is generally believed to be at least 5,000 years old, but some estimates suggest its roots may reach as far back as 10,000 years ago. The oldest known written reference to yoga appears in the ancient Hindu body of texts called the Vedas. (Vedic yoga is based on these texts.) According to legend, the Hindu deity Shiva created hatha yoga, a basic form of yoga that has become very popular in the United States. Yoga was brought to the attention of the Western world in the mid-nineteenth century, along with other aspects of Indian philosophy and tradition.

USES

Yoga is practiced worldwide, in homes, parks, gyms, studios, and various other venues. There are endless yoga videos available online that you can incorporate into your home practice, but if you're new to yoga, it is best to start with a class taught by a certified yoga instructor. Hatha yoga is a basic form that offers all the yoga basics without too many challenging asanas, or postures, making it great for beginners. Kundalini yoga, which focuses on awakening and channeling energy throughout the body, includes chanting, meditation, and breathing techniques in addition to postures. Ashtanga is a physically demanding style that generates heat in the body—and lots of sweat! This type of yoga is great for those who are more fitness focused.

10

The Power of Touch

As one of the five senses (along with sight, hearing, smell, and taste), touch is one of the fundamental parts of human life. We use touch to relate to one another and to experience the world around us, and the simple act of touching or being touched has proven extremely powerful in the realm of health and well-being—both physical and emotional. Each of the practices discussed in this chapter uses touch in a different way. Acupressure involves putting physical pressure on specific points of the body with the aim of relieving pain. Massage includes rubbing techniques designed to promote relaxation, increase circulation, and relieve sore muscles. Reiki is a method in which a practitioner places the palms of his or her hands on different parts of the patient's body with the intent of transferring healing energy. The other topics you'll learn about in this chapter are acupuncture, reflexology, and Rolfing.

Acupressure

ORIGINS

Acupressure is a traditional Chinese medicine technique that has been adopted by the Western world as a form of alternative medicine. Closely related to massage and acupuncture (see entry in this chapter), acupressure is based on the concept that energy flows through "meridians" in the body. It is believed that putting physical pressure on certain points—such as the fleshy web between the thumb and index finger—can clear energy blockages in these meridians and thereby restore or maintain health.

HISTORY/LORE

Although the Chinese have been practicing acupressure for over 5,000 years, and other Asian countries such as India and Japan have their own ancient versions, this technique was unknown to the Western world until the seventeenth century, when it was first introduced in Europe. It wasn't until the 1970s that the practice really took hold in the United States.

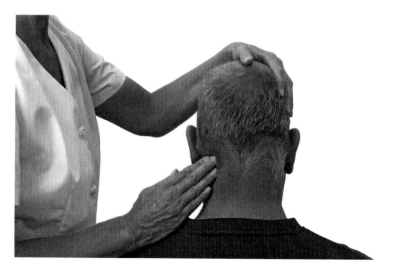

USES

Have you ever found yourself rubbing your temples when you have a head-ache? If so, then you're already familiar with acupressure. This ancient practice has been shown to be enormously effective at relieving pain and discomfort re-sulting from stress, injury, and chronic conditions such as arthritis, even when other options, such as prescription drugs, have failed. But acupressure is not just for those seeking to treat a specific ailment. Many people partake in this prac-tice regularly, similar to massage, to increase circulation, release tension, and maintain general health. If you're interested in giving it a try, you have the op-tion of self-treatment or making an appointment with a certified acupressurist. Information about both is available online.

Acupuncture

ORIGINS

Much like acupressure (see entry in this chapter), acupuncture is a traditional Chinese medicine technique that is now used worldwide. The difference between the two? Needles. Acupuncture targets the same pressure points used in acupressure, but instead of applying physical pressure to those points, fine needles are inserted into the skin. But don't be alarmed; the needles are so tiny that typically you don't even feel them. The word *acupuncture* comes from the Latin *acus*, meaning "needle," and *pungere*, meaning "to prick."

HISTORY/LORE

The exact timeline of acupuncture is unknown, but it is believed to have developed out of the practice of acupressure somewhere between 2,000 and 4,000 years ago. Many Americans first learned about acupuncture by reading an article written by the journalist James Reston (1909–1995) that was published in the *New York Times* in July 1971. Reston wrote about his experience of having an appendectomy while visiting China and being treated with acupuncture for the pain following the surgery.

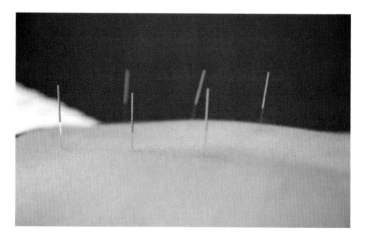

USES

While traditionally acupuncture was believed to be effective due to its interaction with chi (the "life force") and meridians of energy, modern medicine has revealed that the practice stimulates the signaling systems of the body, including the nervous system, which is responsible for the way pain registers in our brains. Like acupressure, acupuncture has proven an effective technique for pain relief in cases where other remedies have been unsuccessful. Unlike acupressure, this is not something you can experiment with at home. Instead, make an appointment with a certified acupuncturist. While most people end up trying acupuncture as a last resort, it's better to give it a try earlier in the process so that you can avoid the possibility of unnecessary surgery, prescription drugs you don't need, and other unpleasant experiences.

Massage

ORIGINS

Massage is an ancient form of bodywork that involves rubbing or kneading parts of the body to aid circulation, induce relaxation, or treat pain and injury. Popular types of massage include Swedish massage, deep tissue massage, and hot stone massage. The word *massage* comes from the Arabic *masaha*, meaning "to stroke, anoint."

HISTORY/LORE

Evidence suggests that most of the ancient civilizations practiced massage, from the Egyptians to the Chinese. The ancient Greek physician Hippocrates (c. 460–c. 370 B.C.E.), who is often referred to as the "father of Western medicine," wrote extensively about massage, stating, "the physician must be experienced in many things, but assuredly also in rubbing." Pehr Henrik Ling (1766–1839), who pioneered the teaching of physical education in Sweden, is often called the "father of Swedish massage"; however, others claim "Swedish massage" is actually a misnomer and its true creator was Johann Georg Mezger (1838–1909), a Dutch physician who incorporated massage into his practice in the second half of the nineteenth century.

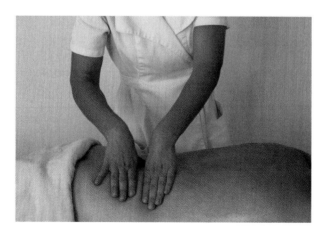

USES

Massage is both a wonderfully relaxing experience and a tried-and-true method of easing pain and discomfort. There are many self-massage techniques that you can experiment with on your own, but for the full massage experience, make an appointment with a certified massage therapist. There are lots of different types of massage you can try. Swedish massage, which involves long strokes, circular pressure, and stretching, is what most people in the Western world think of when they think of massage. Deep tissue massage is similar to Swedish massage but focuses on the deeper layers of muscle tissue, tendons, and connective tissue. In a hot stone massage, a massage therapist uses heated stones to warm and relax the muscles.

Reflexology

ORIGINS

The term *reflexology* has two meanings. It is both the study of the reflexes of the body and how they affect behavior, and a massage technique that involves finger pressure, particularly applied to the hands and feet. The basis of this alternative medicine technique is related to the foundations of acupressure and acupuncture (see entries in this chapter). Practitioners believe certain points on the hands and feet correspond to different areas of the body, and that introducing pressure to those areas can treat ailments and conditions that manifest elsewhere.

HISTORY/LORE

Modern reflexology has its roots in various ancient bodywork practices, including acupressure and massage. Though the practice was not documented in any specific way until relatively recently, there is significant evidence that reflexology was practiced by a number of ancient civilizations. In Egypt's Saqqara burial ground, the Tomb of Ankhmahor, also known as the "Physician's Tomb," which dates back to 2330 B.C.E., includes an image that depicts two men having their hands and feet massaged.

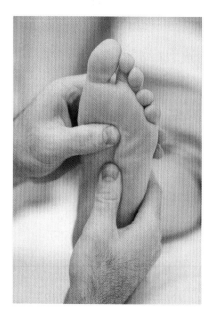

USES

Like other forms of massage, reflexology is something anyone can try, either on their own or with a certified specialist. There are lots of resources available on-line, from self-treatment techniques to listings of reflexologists in your area. The Reflexology Association of America, a nonprofit member organization whose mission is "to elevate and standardize the quality of reflexology services available to the public," offers lots of information on its website (*http://reflexology-usa.org*). The International Institute of Reflexology website (*www.reflexology-usa.net*) is another great resource, with reflexology charts and a list of trained reflexologists by state.

Reiki

ORIGINS

Reiki is a Japanese alternative medicine technique in which a practitioner places the palms of his or her hands on (or above) specific areas of the patient's body as a way of transferring energy to the patient for the purposes of healing. The practice is based on the Chinese principle of chi (or qi), the "life force." The word *Reiki* comes from the Mandarin *língqì*, which is a combination of "numinous spirit" and "energy."

HISTORY/LORE

The Japanese Buddhist Mikao Usui (1865–1926) is known as the creator of Reiki. According to the inscription on his memorial stone, erected in 1927, Usui taught Reiki to more than 2,000 people during his lifetime. Hawayo Takata (1900–1980), a Japanese-American woman born in Hawaii, is credited with introducing Reiki to the Western world. Her teacher, Dr. Chujiro Hayashi (1880–1940), was trained by Usui in the early 1900s.

USES

The practice of Reiki is available to anyone and can be learned with time and practice. There are many self-treatment methods you can try, or you can visit a certified Reiki practitioner. A Reiki session is similar to a massage: The patient lies on a table and spends time both face up and face down so the practitioner can access both sides of the body. Unlike massage, the patient is typically fully clothed. Reiki treats the whole person, including the body, mind, emotions, and spirit. In addition to the myriad health benefits, it is also a wonderful relaxation technique.

Rolfing

ORIGINS

Rolfing is an alternative medical treatment defined by the Rolf Institute of Structural Integration as "a form of hands-on manipulation and movement" that "works on the web-like network of connective tissues, called fascia, to release, realign and balance the whole body, potentially resolving discomfort, reducing compensations and alleviating pain." As a guest on *The Oprah Winfrey Show* in 2007, the Turkish-American surgeon, author, and TV personality Mehmet Oz (born 1960), also known as Dr. Oz, described Rolfing as "even deeper than deep tissue massage."

HISTORY/LORE

Rolfing is named for Ida Rolf (1896–1979), an American biochemist who, in the 1940s, developed structural integration, a type of bodywork that focuses on the connective tissue that surrounds the muscles, blood vessels, organs, and nerves of the body. In the 1950s, Rolf and her son Richard taught classes in various locations throughout the United States. The Rolf Institute of Structural Integration, founded in 1971 and based in Boulder, Colorado, has produced more than 1,500 practitioners of Rolf's techniques.

USES

Rolfing is not as popular or widespread as some of the other practices covered in this chapter, but you may still be able to find a certified Rolfer in your area. The Rolf Institute of Structural Integration's website (*www.rolf.org*) offers lots of great information as well as a search function to find a Rolfer by location.

Glossary

absolute: in aromatherapy, an extract obtained through the use of chemical solvents

adaptogen: a natural substance that helps the body adapt to stress and assists in normalizing bodily processes

aphrodisiac: something, such as an herb or a food, that arouses or intensifies sexual desire

aromatherapy: the use of fragrant materials or substances, such as herbs and essential oils, to affect one's mood and promote overall health and well-being

astral body: a supersensible body that survives the death of the physical body and is capable of ascending or traveling to other realms of consciousness

bodywork: the use of physical therapy techniques, such as massage, for the purpose of enhancing physical and emotional health and well-being

botanist: one who studies or works with plants

chakras: the energy centers of the body, arranged along the spine

chi: an ancient Chinese principle that represents the life force believed to be present in all things; often referred to in traditional Chinese medicine

counterirritant: a remedy that causes irritation at the surface to relieve a deeper source of irritation

deciduous: a plant or tree that loses its leaves at the end of the growing season

divination: the practice of foretelling future events through supernatural means

evergreen: a plant or tree with leaves that remain green year-round

expectorant: a remedy that facilitates the removal of phlegm or mucus from the respiratory tract

faeries: magical spirit creatures often depicted as young, winged, human-like beings

feng shui: the ancient Chinese practice of positioning objects in a way that facilitates a free flow of energy

genera: plural of *genus*

genus: in biology, a category designating a group of species that are closely related and usually exhibit similar characteristics; in a scientific name, the genus is capitalized and italicized

heartwood: the older inner wood of a tree or shrub; it is typically darker and harder than the younger outer wood (called sapwood)

insomnia: a sleep disorder characterized by an inability to fall asleep or remain asleep for an adequate amount of time

lucid dream: a dream in which the dreamer is aware that he or she is dreaming

Mesopotamia: an ancient region of southwestern Asia between the Tigris and Euphrates Rivers in modern-day Iraq; home to numerous early civilizations, including the Babylonians and the Sumerians

misnomer: an error in naming a person or place

Mohs scale: a scale for classifying minerals based on hardness; ranges from 1 (softest) to 10 (hardest)

Neolithic era: the period of human history beginning around 8000 B.C.E. characterized by the development of agriculture

note: in aromatherapy, a distinctive component of a complex flavor or aroma

occult: relating to supernatural or magical influences, powers, or events

onomatopoeia: the use of words that imitate the sounds associated with the actions or objects they refer to

out-of-body experience: an experience in which the mind/soul/spirit leaves the physical body and views the body from a higher plane or vantage point; often includes travel to other planes or realms such as the astral plane or spirit realm

Paleolithic era: the period of human history that began about 2.4 million years ago and lasted until between 15,000 and 11,500 years ago; also known as the Stone Age due to the early stone tools that have been found dating back to this period

panacea: a remedy for all diseases, evils, or difficulties; a cure-all

papyrus: a paper-like material made of plant pith used by ancient civilizations as a surface for writing and painting

poultice: a soft, moist, heated mass placed on an inflamed or irritated part of the body to stimulate or soothe it

raceme: a stalk of a flowering plant with flowers arranged singly along an unbranched axis; from the Latin *racemus*, meaning "a bunch of grapes"

Raynaud's disease: a circulatory condition caused by insufficient blood supply to the hands and feet; named after the French physician Maurice Raynaud (1834–1881)

reincarnation: the rebirth of the soul (or spirit or consciousness) in another body after death

resin: a substance secreted by a plant or tree that heals wounds and protects the plant or tree against disease

scrying: the practice of gleaning information from images "seen" in a reflective, translucent, or luminescent surface, such as water or a crystal

smudging: the process of using directed smoke to cleanse a person, object, or area

taxonomy: a system of classifying and naming organisms that indicates natural relationships; the Swedish botanist Carl Linnaeus (1707–1778) is known as the father of modern taxonomy

totem: an animal, plant, or object serving as an emblem of a group of people such as a family or clan

umbel: a flat-topped or rounded cluster of flowers; characteristic of plants in the parsley family

Wicca: a Neopagan religion based on the practice of ceremonial witchcraft; developed in England during the first half of the twentieth century

Index